EAST DOCK CARDIFF.

THE
CARDIFF RAILWAY

by
Eric R. Mountford

THE OAKWOOD PRESS

© The Oakwood Press and E. R. Mountford 1987
ISBN 0 85361 347 8
Printed and bound by S&S Press, Abingdon, Oxford

Acknowledgements

The author wishes to acknowledge and thank the individuals and public bodies that readily assisted by providing records, or relating personal recollections, during the research stage of this project.

In particular his thanks are due to: The Public Record Office (British Transport Historical Records), Kew; The Central Reference Library, Cardiff; The Welsh Industrial and Maritime Museum, Cardiff; British Rail (Western Region) South Wales Divisional HQ, Cardiff; British Rail (Western Region) District Civil Engineer's Office, Newport; Associated British Ports (South Wales Group) Cardiff; The Railway Correspondence and Travel Society's publication "Locomotives of the GWR", Part 10; "Country Life", 18th September, 1980, article by Bryan Little. Also to Mr Alan Care, of Cardiff, whose excellent recollections provided much of the data re the locomotive and train working on the Cardiff Railway section in the early years following the amalgamation with the GWR in 1922, to Mr D.S.M. Barrie and to Steve Jones.

The author is also grateful to the many photographers and collectors who have so readily provided the illustrations necessary to enhance and back up the printed word. His particular thanks are due to: Dr Stuart Owen Jones, Asst Keeper of the Welsh I&MM, Cardiff; Francis Equeall; Sid Rickard; John White; Ian Wright; Bob Pugh. All the above supplied several unique pictures without which sufficient cover to the subject could not have been given. The photographic contributions from many other individuals, far too numerous to mention individually, have been just as welcome, and each is credited alongside the photograph(s) he has provided.

To Sue Potts and Julie Kennedy for retyping the manuscript.

Published by
The OAKWOOD PRESS
P.O. Box 122, Headington, Oxford

The Pierhead Building, showing the West Dock (*centre left*) and the East Dock lock entrance (*bottom right*) c.1920.

Welsh Industrial and Maritime Museum, Cardiff

Dedication

For Penny and Jacky

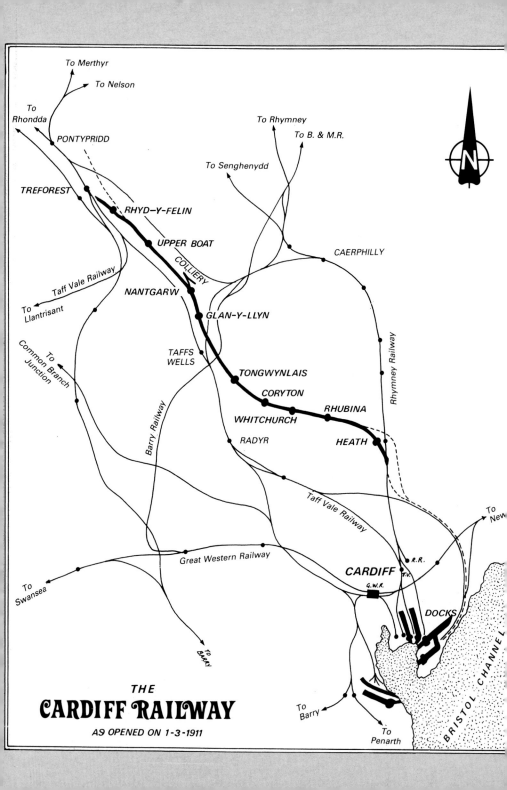

To Merthyr

To Nelson

To Rhondda

PONTYPRIDD

To Rhymney

To B. & M.R.

To Senghenydd

TREFOREST

RHYD-Y-FELIN

UPPER BOAT

CAERPHILLY

COLLIERY

Taff Vale Railway

NANTGARW

To Llantrisant

GLAN-Y-LLYN

Common Branch Junction

To

TAFFS WELLS

Rhymney Railway

Barry Railway

TONGWYNLAIS

CORYTON

RHUBINA

WHITCHURCH

RADYR

HEATH

Taff Vale Railway

To New

Great Western Railway

R.R.

To Swansea

CARDIFF

T.V.

G.W.R.

DOCKS

TO BARAY

THE
CARDIFF RAILWAY
AS OPENED ON 1-3-1911

To Barry

To Penarth

BRISTOL CHANNEL

THE CARDIFF RAILWAY

Contents

Introduction

Despite its name, the Cardiff Railway Company controlled one of the great seaports of the world, whereas the railway the company planned to feed it was insignificant in comparison, never achieved its aim, and was largely closed just twenty years after its opening. Nevertheless its history is full of interest, particularly the long standing disputes with the Taff Vale Railway, who were not only far too clever for the Cardiff babes of the railway industry, but also for Parliament, which had authorised the Cardiff's aim to bring much of its traffic to its docks themselves, an aim continually frustrated by the TVR moves to prevent fruition. The railway was also unusual in that seventeen years after its closure, the rusty, weed overgrown, rails of the northern section, suddenly sprang back into life as an outlet for Nantgarw Colliery, then being developed by the NCB, and part of the formerly closed section is still in use for that purpose today.

In the matter of confrontation with the TVR the railway was merely following what had already been the case at the docks almost since its opening in 1839. Apart from brief periods when the two parties were jointly threatened by a third party (i.e. the Barry Dock and Railway), they were almost continually in conflict, and the railway disputes were merely a continuation.

It is a tragedy that the Docks and the TVR were not amalgamated as first mooted in the mid-1840s, and almost every decade afterwards. If so, this story would have been entirely different. As it was, despite Cardiff Docks being well known in every corner of the earth, and dealing with tonnages (mostly steam coal export) that were the envy of almost every other port, it never produced the dividends for the Marquis of Bute, and other shareholders, that should have resulted from the enormous capital expenditure incurred, and the vast amount of trade which resulted, whilst the railway was nothing short of a costly disaster for the company.

John, second Marquis of Bute 1793–1848, founder of Cardiff Docks which, in turn, created modern Cardiff.   *Welsh Industrial and Maritime Museum, Cardiff*

Part One
The Bute Docks, Cardiff

The port of Cardiff developed as the natural outlet for the products from the industrial region of NE Glamorganshire, initially for the iron trade from the furnaces in the Merthyr Tydfil area, soon followed by a bituminous coal trade from the lower Rhondda Valley, the Taff Valley and the Gellygaer area. From the mid-nineteenth century there was an increasing demand for the high quality steam coal mined initially in the Aberdare Valley but from the 1870s onwards more particularly from the Rhondda Valleys, and to a lesser extent from the Rhymney Valley.

In the later eighteenth century the trade had been comparatively small, and was transported down to the coast by pack mule and shipped at small wharves located near the mouth of the River Taff, about one mile south of Cardiff which, apart from its castle, was virtually unknown at the time, and had a population of less than 1000 people.

By the 1790s trade had increased sufficiently to justify the cutting of the Glamorganshire Canal from Merthyr to Cardiff, opened in February 1794. Four years later a basin, for the better accommodation of the shipping, was opened at the southern extremity of the canal near its entrance to the Bristol Channel. However the trade continued to expand, and it soon became obvious that the canal was not the answer to the transportation problem. During its 24½ miles of length there were no less than 49 locks to cover the rise to Merthyr, some 543 feet, causing endless delay. By the early 1820s congestion on the canal was a serious problem and, coupled with bank bursts and resultant loss of water, and with freezing in the Winter, delays were regular and even in the best conditions barges were taking about three days to complete the journey.

A scheme was prepared to extend the Merthyr to Abercynon tram road to Cardiff, but nothing came of that. In the late 1820s the second Marquis of Bute, an extensive landowner in the Cardiff and its valleys areas, was approached to consider constructing a dock at Cardiff capable of catering for ocean going shipping as, at that time the export trade was loaded into coastal craft at the canal Basin, shipped to Bristol and trans-shipped there into ocean going vessels. Hence on 16th July, 1830 the Marquis obtained an Act of Parliament authorising such dock, or ship canal, as it was then called. Initially he made no move to start construction, biding his time until improved transport arrangements between the valleys and Cardiff had reached the same stage.

In 1834 things began to move, the traffic had increased by leaps and bounds and delays on the canal had got worse, hence the Merthyr

7

1 WILL. IV.—Sess. 1830.

A N

A   C   T

For empowering the Marquis of *Bute*, to make and maintain a Ship Canal, commencing near the Mouth of the River *Taff*, in the County of *Glamorgan*, and terminating near the Town of *Cardiff*, with other Works to communicate therewith.

[ROYAL ASSENT, 16 *July* 1830.]

WHEREAS the making and maintaining a Ship Canal, to commence at a certain point or place called *The Eastern Hollows*, at or near the mouth of the River *Taff*, in the County of *Glamorgan*, and to terminate in a northern or north-easterly direction towards the Town of *Cardiff*, in *Cardiff* Moors; and also the establishing and constructing a Wet Dock or Basin and other Works, at the termination of the said Ship Canal, near the said Town of *Cardiff*; and also the making and maintaining one · or more Cuts out of and from the said Wet Dock or Basin, to communicate with the *Glamorganshire* Canal, together with Sluices or Tunnels, Piers and other Works joining and communicating with the said Ship Canal, Wet Dock or Basin, Cuts and other Works, will, by avoiding the dangers and difficulties of the present intricate Navigation from the Sea to the said *Glamorganshire* Canal, and by affording additional accommodation and security to ships and other vessels, materially increase and improve the Trade and Commerce of the said Town of *Cardiff* and its neighbourhood ; and by facilitating the exportation of Mineral and other Produce,

Preamble. Expediency of forming a Ship Canal, Wet Dock, and other Works.

The first page of the 1830 Act which authorised the Marquis of Bute to construct his first dock at Cardiff, later known as the Bute West Dock.

Aerial photograph of Cardiff Docks 1950. The Queen Alexandra Dock is in the foreground, with the Roath Dock (*centre right*) and the West and East Docks (*centre left*). *Associated British Ports (South Wales Group)*

ironmasters (apart from Crawshay of the Cyfarthfa works who was virtually in control of the canal) called in Brunel to make a survey and estimate for a railway from Merthyr to Cardiff, and the Marquis obtained a second Act dated 22nd May, 1834 to modify the dock scheme in relation to prevailing circumstances, and work was started in December of that year. The initial Bill presented in November 1834 for a Cardiff to Merthyr Railway was not proceeded with, but the following year a second Bill was deposited, resulting in the Taff Vale Railway Act of inauguration on 21st June, 1836. About 30% of the capital for the railway came from speculators in Bristol, who feared that the new railway and dock would have a disastrous effect on the port of Bristol, they being unable to put their money into the Bute Dock concern as this was a private enterprise by the Marquis himself.

The dock opened on 9th October, 1839 with the first vessel – the *Lady Charlotte*, named after the wife of the principal ironmaster in the Merthyr area, Sir John Guest of Dowlais – and it is recorded that in her excitement at the opening ceremony the real Lady Charlotte leaped from the quayside on to the ship's deck, quickly followed by many of the other guests, causing not only the ship to have a bad list, but with most of those present being part of the opening ceremony and not spectators as planned.

It was almost a year later that the first section of the railway opened, on 8th October, 1840 from Navigation (Abercynon) to Cardiff, but already the first shadows were clouding the initial harmonious relationship between the Marquis and the TVR. From the beginning the Taff would have preferred to have been a dock owning railway company, and in their initial Act had obtained authority to construct a branch railway to the west bank of the River Ely, to the west of the Bute dock, on which site Brunel was instructed on 16th September, 1836 to prepare plans for a harbour. During the next three or four years the Marquis called in expert opinion, particularly Robert Stephenson as a Consulting Engineer, to assure himself that the siting of the proposed Ely dock was not as good as his own dock site. Having re-assured himself negotiations were started with the TVR. The Marquis naturally wanted the Ely scheme abandoned, at the same time he wanted his own dock to be equally available for all traders, whereas the Taff insisted on the exclusive use of most of the west side of the dock. During negotiations the Taff, on 2nd November, 1840 opened a siding running down that side, but it was not until March 1842 that an agreement was signed. This included the Taff's demands in return for which the railway company agreed not to proceed with the Ely branch and harbour, nor ship at their own canal dock (the Little Dock) which the Taff had acquired in 1837/8 to receive the materials and plant necessary for the construction of their railway.

Regular traffic of iron and coal started on the Taff in June 1841, and initially such traffic had to be manhandled in barrows between rail wagon and ship. Early in December 1842 the Taff erected the first mechanical coaling appliance at the dock, the remaining appliances necessary being completed by the summer of 1843. These merely lifted the wagon, swung it over the ship's hold, and tilted it to allow the coal to descend. A small amount of coal was manhandled into coastal vessels in the Little Dock, the Marquis agreeing to same on the condition that the Taff paid him the same wharfage dues as would have applied if the coal had been shipped at his own dock.

Later in 1843 the Marquis and the TVR made a provisional agreement (the first of several) for the railway company to purchase, or lease, his dock and a Bill was put forward for the 1844 Session to authorise this. However, the TVR wanted to cut out all opposition by acquiring the Glamorganshire Canal also, but as negotiations between the latter parties broke down in December 1843 the Marquis withdrew from his side of the agreement leaving the Taff to delete all reference to the proposed lease, or sale, from their Bill.

Nevertheless the Marquis, fully realising that he needed the TVR as much as they needed his dock, made a further provisional agreement with the railway on 17th May, 1844, which resulted in a Heads of Arrangement between the parties dated 21st October, 1844, in which the non financial clauses were –

a) The Marquis to lease the east side of the dock to the TVR for 250 years for coal shipment, the west side to be used for general trade.

b) The TVR to abandon the Ely harbour and branch.

c) The TVR to ship, as far as they are able, all minerals and goods at the Bute Dock.

With the approval of the Marquis the Taff promoted a further Bill for the 1845 Session seeking authorisation for the sale or lease of the dock to the TVR. Unfortunately this Bill was not presented within the time limit imposed by Parliament and automatically failed. The parties agreed to promote a similar Bill for the following Session but, once again, the Marquis changed his mind and advised the Taff that he would prefer to stand by the 1844 agreement. The Taff, fed up with the Marquis's changes of mind, decided to ensure the legality of the agreement by including it as a schedule in their 1845/6 Bill, hence it became law by the TVR Act of 26th August, 1846.

Meanwhile the Marquis, who until 1845 had personally handled the negotiations, set up a Trust on 20th February, 1845 to manage his dock, lands and mineral rights in the South Wales area, with the proviso that during his lifetime he could veto any of their decisions. The Trust arrangement was included in his Will dated 22nd July, 1847 which the Marquis only survived a few months, as he died at his home, Cardiff Castle, on 18th March, 1848.

Having to move from the west to the east side of the dock following the 1844 agreement proved a blessing in disguise for the Taff. A new type of hydraulic coal tipping appliance had been designed whereby the wagon was fed into the tip at high level, tilted and the coal discharged into the ship by an extended shute. Hence it was decided to construct the branch to the east side of the dock (the East Branch) on the high level. Construction was well advanced when the Marquis died, and the first new tip was successfully tested on 22nd July, 1848 when a train of coal, from Cymmer Colliery, was tipped into the vessel *Mayflower*. The branch was not officially opened until 4th December, 1848 by which time the Taff had erected eight such tips, five of which were reserved for the traffic from leading individual colliery owners, the other three for coal from the smaller collieries. Three of the old type coal lifts were removed from the west side of the dock and re-erected at the Little Dock, the others were removed and dismantled.

To confirm their position in law the Trustees obtained the Marquis of Bute Estate Act of 31st August, 1848. At the time the late Marquis's only son was less than one year old, and the Act authorised the Trustees control until the third Marquis came of age. At this stage the relationship between the Trustees and the TVR was cordial but, in the changed circumstances, it was thought desirable for a new agreement to be drawn up, and this was signed on 1st December, 1849. This was generally in accordance with the 1844 agreement except that the Trustees inserted a clause that should the TVR ship at any other port, where they had the control of such traffic, the same wharfage dues should be paid to the Trustees as if shipped at the Bute Dock. At the time the Taff could not envisage any problems from such clause, they had already abandoned their Ely harbour scheme and were already paying such dues for the small amount of coal shipped at their Little Dock.

However, the situation changed completely during the next four years. The broad gauge South Wales Railway opened their east to west route through Cardiff on 18th June, 1850 and started negotiations with the Trustees for access to the dock. By that time the dock was congested with the existing traffic hence in the agreement, signed 31st March, 1851, the Trustees agreed to construct a second more modern dock, to which the SWR would have access. The Taff

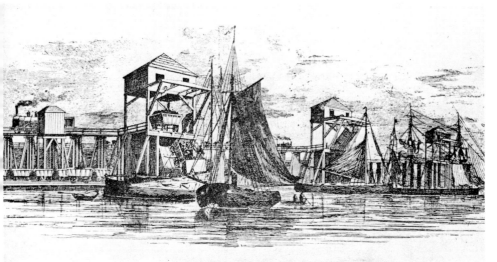

COAL SHIPPING AT CARDIFF. 1850.

Looking across the (West) Dock in 1850, showing the high level coaling branch (the East Branch). *Welsh Industrial and Maritime Museum, Cardiff*

TVR 0–6–0 *Newbridge* (Hick & Co. 1846) alongside the dock. (This photograph was dated 1849, and thus could be one of the oldest known railway photographs.) *Late E.R. Baker*

had no objection as they incorrectly assumed that their 1849 agreement would be amended to give them usage of the new dock. This may well have been the case but for the advent of a third railway, the Rhymney. Apart from the Rhymney iron works and its associated collieries, the Rhymney valley had not been developed to the extent of the valleys served by the Taff, and the new railway (authorised in 1854) was originally intended as a feeder to the TVR, in much the same way as the Aberdare Railway had been in 1846. However, on 2nd July, 1855 the RR obtained a second Act which altered the situation. This extended their railway down the valley to the Caerphilly area, from where it would cross into the Taff valley and connect with the TVR at Walnut Tree Jn, Taffs Well, several miles further south than the originally intended Llancaiach Jn. The same Act also authorised a separate branch to the new dock, leaving the Taff at Crockherbtown Jn just north of that company's Cardiff passenger station. Compared to the 1854 Act this deprived the Taff not only of some 11½ miles of expected revenue earning traffic, but also of the terminal and shipping charges at the dock. This led to extreme bitterness between the two railway companies not all of which is part of the docks story. For further details the reader should refer to D.S. Barrie's individual histories of the two companies concerned.

However, some of the bitterest feuds took place within the dock area. John Boyle, one of the original promoters of the RR and its Chairman until his death late in the nineteenth century, was appointed as one of the Trustees in April 1852, and soon became the managing trustee. Boyle disliked the TVR and, as head of the RR and the docks interests, he waged a continuous battle against that company for many years, both within the dock area and in the valleys. As ocean-going vessels were getting progressively larger, the Trustees, in 1853, decided to make the second dock deeper than originally planned, and it was fixed at 25 feet, whereas the old dock had a depth of 19 feet for about half of its length, and only 13 feet for the remainder. Boyle determined that the RR would get the most advantageous sites at the new dock and, as far as possible, confine the TVR to the old dock. He also arranged for the coal shipping appliances at the new dock to be installed by the Trustees and leased to the railway companies, again for the benefit of the RR who could ill afford to construct these themselves.

The new Bute East Dock was part opened on 20th July, 1855, the old dock then being known as the Bute West Dock. The SWR had opened their broad gauge branch to the dock on 17th January, 1854 and were allotted three coal tips near the southern end at the east side. The TVR were also allotted three tips at the extreme south end

RR 0–6–0ST No. 53 alongside the East Dock c.mid 1890s. (Note HL and LL sidings.)
Locomotive Publishing Co.

TVR 0–6–0ST No. 263 near one of the timber yards at the docks c.mid 1890s.
L&GRP, Courtesy David & Charles

on the opposite side, to which they laid a short connection from their East branch. The RR was still then under construction, but had already made agreement with the Trustees for the sole use of all other tips at the dock, which itself was only part completed. A tidal harbour for coastal shipping opened on 13th August, 1856, this sited a short distance south of the East Dock, and once again the RR secured an agreement for its sole use for the coal trade. As this harbour was opened well before the RR was ready, the Trustees reluctantly granted the TVR temporary usage of its tips, but only on the clear understanding that, once the RR was completed, all coal for shipment at the tidal harbour had to be handed over to that company at Crockherbtown Jn for conveyance to the harbour, and shipped by the RR.

The RR's docks branch opened in December 1857 and, until its main line opened throughout on 25th February, 1858, was used on a temporary basis by the TVR for coal shipment on the east side of the East Dock and at the tidal harbour. The dock itself was completed by extensions opened on 19th January, 1858 and 14th September, 1859 and from that date the RR had almost complete domination at the new dock. As from 14th June, 1859 the Trustees further assisted the RR by opening a new high level branch, known as the Viaduct branch, which looped around the north end of the East Dock, and then down the west side, over which the RR were allowed to ferry their coal to the tips on that side, apart from the three worked by the TVR at the southern end. At that stage Boyle relaxed happily as far as the docks were concerned. Despite the negligible coal traffic then mined in the Rhymney Valley, his railway company now controlled eleven of the seventeen deep water tips at the East Dock, plus the seven at the tidal harbour for coastal vessels, whereas the Taff controlled but three deep water tips, along with the West Dock tips which were then only suitable for coastal trade. By that time most of the Taff's ever increasing steam coal traffic was for export and, as the three tips allotted were hopelessly inadequate to cope, Boyle well knew that a considerable part of such traffic would have to be handed over to the RR at Crockherbtown Jn for that company to convey to the docks and ship. This had all been achieved without any loss of revenue to the Trustees, who received their dock dues whoever handled the traffic. Boyle was a happy man.

Statistics for the year 1860, the first complete year after the East Dock had been opened, illustrate how Boyle had considerably increased RR revenue at no loss to the Trustees, but seriously to the detriment of the TVR.

Taff Vale Railway – 19 coal tips available
  7 at the West Dock (water depth 19 feet) ⎫ suitable for
  6 at the West Dock (water depth 13 feet) ⎬ coastal trade
  3 at the Little Dock ⎭ only (16)
  3 at the East Dock (water depth 25 feet) for foreign trade
Coal brought to Cardiff for shipment 1,731,817 tons.

Rhymney Railway – 18 coal tips available
  11 at the East Dock (water depth 25 feet) for foreign trade
  7 at the Tidal Harbour for coastal trade.
Coal brought to Cardiff for shipment 88,319 tons.

Coal handed over by the TVR to the RR at Crockherbtown Jn 698,920 tons.

Even this did not completely satisfy John Boyle. As the East Dock (and the Tidal Harbour) had been privately constructed on the Marquis' land without the need of a Parliamentary Act, the Trustees alone could decide its usage, and did everything possible to prevent the TVR using the three deep water tips which they had been allotted This resulted in an even greater percentage of TVR coal having to be handed over to the RR for shipment as the following summary for 1855–1864 illustrates.

Year	TVR coal	RR coal	TVR coal handed over to RR	Coal shipped by TVR
1855	980,632	–	–	980,632
1857	1,256,213	–	–	1,256,213
1859	1,462,718	45,758	411,692	1,051,026
1861	1,701,731	166,000	860,403	841,328
1864	1,903,235	197,467	1,180,657	722,578

Thus in 1864 the TVR were forced to hand over 60% of their coal traffic to the RR for shipment, amounting to over 85% of the shipment coal traffic handled by the RR! Little wonder the TVR retaliated by petty restrictions on Rhymney traffic passing over Taff metals between Walnut Tree and Crockherbtown Jns, the side of the story usually told.

However, that year saw the TVR fighting back. The ever increasing coal traffic meant a third dock was needed, and during the Parliamentary Session the Trustees sought powers to construct such dock. The Taff seized the opportunity to vigorously oppose on the grounds that there were no provisions in the Bill for access to the proposed dock by their railway. Finally the Trustees were forced to grant such access but set their charges so high that the Taff continued to oppose and the Bill was thrown out.

In the 1865 Session the Trustees promoted a similar Bill, which also included provision for bringing the East Dock under Parliamentary,

CR Kitson 0–4–0ST (No. 5 or 6) with train of pit props at the docks *c.*1906.
Welsh Industrial and Maritime Museum, Cardiff

GWR 0–6–0ST No. 1711 shunting at the docks *c.*1906.   *F. Equeall*

CR 0–6–0T No. 30 decorated for the opening of the Queen Alexandra Dock, 13th July, 1907.   *F. Equeall*

CR Parfitt & Jenkins 0–6–0ST shunting one of the timber yards *c*.1908.
                                    Welsh Industrial and Maritime Museum, Cardiff

or lawful, control. As the dock charges were again so high as to be unacceptable to the Taff, they once again managed to get the dock clauses of the Bill rejected, but the section dealing with bringing the East Dock under lawful control was passed by the Bute Dock Act of 5th July, 1865.

With a third dock urgently needed the Trustees were forced to come to a reasonable agreement with the TVR, both in regard to the proposed dock charges and to reasonable access to *all* tips on the west side of the East Dock. Initially the Trustees agreed to construct a junction from their own (1859) high level branch on the west side of the dock, to the almost adjacent TVR's East branch. This was completed on 19th July, 1865 but the Taff were not to be allowed use of same until the third dock Bill had become law. On their side the TVR insisted on a clause being inserted in the Bill legalising the agreement giving them access to the tips on the west side. Unfortunately for the Trustees the Bute Docks Act of 30th July, 1866 did not authorise the major dock they sought, but merely a basin, whilst the TVR's use of the west side tips was legalised. In the circumstances the Trustees could only delay the TVR from using the newly constructed junction, which they managed to do until 29th April, 1867.

The continued feuding between the TVR and RR over docks usage made the Trustees realise that it was time they handled the tips and tip roads themselves, hence in the same Act they obtained authority to construct their own railway to the new basin (the Roath Basin) also the tip sidings, and control the actual tipping. The 1866 Act had been a clear victory for the TVR over both the Trustees and the RR, to which the Trustees reacted by devoting themselves increasingly to the working of the dock to the partial exclusion of the railway companies, whilst the RR sought revenge by striking deep into Taff territory (Merthyr, Dowlais, Aberdare etc.) to cream off as much of the lucrative steam coal traffic from those areas that they could obtain.

The 1866 Act included the abandonment of the Tidal Harbour, as construction of the Roath Basin would foul the site, and it was closed in July 1868, although the basin was not completed and opened until 23rd July, 1874. By that time there were 39 coal tips available at the Bute Docks, and with the better distribution of their usage, the TVR had ceased to use their Little Dock for coal shipment after 1873.

Coal export figures for the year 1874 clearly reveal how the TVR had regained control of the tipping situation as a result of the 1866 Act.

Total coal exported at Bute Docks   2,583,665 tons (TVR, RR and GWR)
Coal brought to docks by TVR   2,115,588 tons

The Taff's coal was shipped as below:

	Tons	
West Dock	751,252	Direct
East Dock (west side)	1,357,828	Direct
East Dock (east side)	1,040	By RR via Crockherbtown Jn
Roath Basin	5,468	By Trustees via dock sidings

Relations between the Taff and Rhymney Railways were so hostile that even the small quantity shipped at Roath Basin was handed over to the Trustees on the west side of the East Dock, for them to convey over their dock lines to the basin, rather than the more direct method of passing it on to the RR at Crockherbtown Jn.

Even so matters between the Trustees and the Taff were by no means cordial, a long legal battle between the two having been concluded only the previous year. In the early days of the RR–TVR struggle for power at the docks, a number of influential coal and land owners had got together and promoted a railway from the TVR at Penarth Jn (Radyr) to a tidal harbour on the east bank of the River Ely, a somewhat similar scheme to that abandoned by the TVR under their 1844 agreement with the second Marquis. Having obtained authorisation by an Act in 1856, the following year the Company was re-formed as the Penarth Harbour Dock and Railway and, by their Act of 27th July, 1857, obtained powers to construct a dock on the opposite bank of the Ely. The tidal harbour opened for coal shipment on 1st July, 1859 and Penarth Dock on 10th June, 1865. By the PHD&R Co's Leasing Act of 22nd June, 1863 the dock, harbour and railway was leased to the TVR for a term of 999 years, confirming an agreement reached between the parties dated 13th August, 1862.

At that time, it will be recalled, the TVR were in dire conflict with the Trustees re their usage of the Bute East Dock, and the Penarth lease gave them an alternative outlet for their export coal trade. Naturally the Trustees demanded wharfage dues on all coal shipped at Penarth in accordance with the 1849 agreement. The Taff refused to pay claiming that the Penarth undertaking was not their property, they only leased and managed it on behalf of the Penarth Co. and had no control of what coal was shipped there, in the same way that they did not control the coal that colliery companies sent to Southampton or Birkenhead for shipment. The Trustees saw it in a different light altogether; the Penarth Co. was managed by the TVR from the Taff head office, and the TVR ran the trains to and from the dock and harbour direct from the collieries, exactly the same as if it had been part of the Taff system. In the Trustees' view this was entirely a different matter to handing over to another railway to convey the traffic to a port in another part of the country.

The *Terra Nova*, Captain Scott's Antarctic exploration vessel, berthed on the west side of the East Dock, 15th June, 1910, prior to leaving on the ill-fated expedition. *Welsh Industrial and Maritime Museum, Cardiff*

Loaded private owner coal wagons at Roath Storage Sidings, March 1927. (This was fourteen years after the peak year of the export steam coal trade had passed.) *British Rail*

Loading the frame and wheels of 4–6–0 No. 6000 *King George V* on the deck of the steamer *Chicago City*, at the Roath Dock, 3rd August, 1927, *en route* to the Baltimore and Ohio Railway Centenary Exhibition, USA.

Welsh Industrial and Maritime Museum, Cardiff

Off-loading LMS 4–6–2 No. 6220 *Coronation* (actually 6229 renamed/renumbered) from the S.S. *Pacific Pioneer*, at the Queen Alexandra Dock, 16th February, 1942, on its return from America.

Welsh Industrial and Maritime Museum, Cardiff

The dispute passed to the Courts, and after several years of legal wrangling, appeal and cross appeal, eventually ended up for final judgement in the House of Lords. This was given, most reluctantly, in favour of the Taff, Lord Cairns coming to the conclusion that the Penarth undertaking, although leased to the TVR, had been authorised by Parliament as a separate company and, unless amalgamated with the Taff, remained a separate company. In his judgement, delivered on 9th May, 1873, he said, "I cannot help feeling some regret at the result at which I am obliged to arrive. The TVR company have departed in a clear and striking manner from the good faith of the arrangement . . . but have kept themselves from the obligation of the letter of the covenants". The Taff breathed a sigh of relief at the decision, which they knew only too well they had won on a technical point only. When, sixteen years later, the TVR absorbed a number of small satellite railway companies, which they had previously managed or leased, they were careful not to include the Penarth company, as such would have certainly resulted in the Bute interests returning to the Courts with victory virtually assured.

Returning to the Bute Docks, a low water pier for passenger ships plying across the Bristol Channel opened on 16th September, 1868 to coincide with the coming of age of the third Marquis of Bute. A couple of years later a small passenger station opened at the pier, regular trains in connection with the boat services being run from the new Parade Station of the RR, starting on Friday 8th July, 1870. The pier was sited just south of the Roath Basin, then in the very early days of construction, and a dam which had to be constructed closed the entrance to the Tidal Harbour which ceased to function when the pier opened, one coal tip being erected at the land end of the pier to cater for tug boats. The coasters, which formerly called at the Tidal Harbour, had thenceforth to use the docks.

Another railway gained access to the docks the following year. This was the London & North Western Railway which, in return for financial assistance provided to the RR to construct their independent Caerphilly–Cardiff line, were granted running power over the entire RR main line, and commenced through workings via Rhymney Bridge on 2nd October, 1871. The LNWR had their own goods shed and sidings (Tyndall Street) at the north end of the East Dock, an isolated outpost of the Euston empire.

Back at the Bute Docks the continued expansion of the coal export trade called for still another dock. The Roath Basin had certainly eased congestion for a while, but was filled to capacity from the day it opened. Hence on 16th July, 1874 the Trustees obtained an Act to construct a Roath Dock connecting with the basin. Before work had started a severe slump set in following a very lengthy coal strike early in 1875. Several of the iron works and collieries closed permanently, but the coal trade began to recover the following year. The Trustees were not convinced the recovery would last, and made no move to start work on the Roath Dock, which angered the coal owners and shippers, who wrote direct to the third Marquis in an endeavour to get things moving. However, the Marquis felt the time was not ripe to speculate further at his own expense, and also adopted a wait and see attitude.

In the event their decisions were wrong as the export coal trade leapt from just over 2½m tons in 1874 to nearly 5m tons in 1880, and conditions at the Bute Docks became chaotic. Vessels were queuing up to seek entrance to the docks, and inside the ships were so tightly packed that it was said one could walk over the decks from one side of the docks to the other. On the TVR the coal trains followed behind each other all the way from the collieries to the docks, but it was not until 1881 that the Trustees seemed fully aware of the serious situation.

Initially negotiations took place with the aim of selling, or leasing, the entire undertaking to Cardiff Corporation but, as these failed, the Trustees promoted a further Bill for construction of the Roath Dock, and obtained the necessary authorisation in the Bute Docks Act of 18th August, 1882. Despite the massive trade at the docks, the financial returns were very small compared with the profits of the railway companies (the TVR were paying the maximum of 10 per cent plus 7½ per cent bonus in 1882) hence the Trustees had included increased dock charges at the Roath Dock in the Bill. This so angered the coal owners and shippers that they actually opposed the Bill in committee. Due to this, and a chance remark made by the Chairman, the history of the export coal trade in the area was dramatically changed. He asked the freighters why, if they were so opposed to the Trustees Bill, they had not thought of constructing a dock themselves.

Led by David Davies of the Ocean Collieries in the Rhondda, they banded together and had surveys, plans and estimates prepared for a dock at Barry. They presented a Bill for the 1883 Session, not only for such dock but also for an independent railway to it from the Rhondda Valley, at that time the largest coal producing area in the world. The Bute Trustees and the TVR instantly forgot their old enmity and combined to oppose the Bill which, if passed, appeared to be equally disastrous to both. With other opposition they managed to get the Bill thrown out, but the Barry promotors were undaunted and put the measure down again for the following Session. This time they were

[49 & 50 Vict.]   *Bute Docks (Transfer) Act*, 1886.   [**Ch. lxxxvi.**]

CHAPTER lxxxvi.

An Act to incorporate the Bute Docks Company; and to transfer to the Company so incorporated the Bute Docks Undertaking; and for other purposes.   [25th June 1886.]   A.D. 1886.

WHEREAS the Most Honourable John Crichton Stuart, late Marquess of Bute and Earl of Dumfries, now deceased (in this Act called "the late Marquess"), being or claiming to be the owner in fee simple of large estates at Cardiff and elsewhere in the county of Glamorgan, and being interested in the prosperity of the town and port of Cardiff and the neighbourhood thereof obtained an Act of the first year of William the Fourth, chapter one hundred and thirty-three, intituled "An Act for empowering "the Marquis of Bute to make and maintain a ship canal com- "mencing near the mouth of the River Taff in the county of "Glamorgan and terminating near the town of Cardiff with other "works to communicate therewith," (herein-after called "the Dock Act of 1830"); which Act was amended by an Act of the fourth year of William the Fourth chapter nineteen, (herein-after called "the Dock Act of 1834"):   *Bute Dock Acts of 1830 and 1834.*   *1 Will. 4. c. cxxxiii.*   *4 Will. 4. c. xix.*

And whereas by an indenture dated the twentieth day of February one thousand eight hundred and forty-five the late Marquess conveyed his lands at or near Cardiff, including the ship canal harbour docks and things to which he was entitled under the said Acts, to trustees upon trust for raising moneys as therein mentioned, and with the powers of leasing management improvement and superintendence, and of dealing and contracting, therein expressed; and the said indenture contained a declaration that on the decease of the said Marquess the trusts of that deed should cease unless or to such extent only as he should by will direct, and that in such event the harbour and hereditaments comprised therein should be held by the trustees in trust for his heirs and assigns as if that deed had never been made: *Trust deed of 1845.*

And whereas the late Marquess by his will dated the twenty-second day of July one thousand eight hundred and forty-seven   *Will of the late Marquess, and*

[*Local.*—86.]

The first page of the 1886 Act which incorporated the Bute Docks Company.

successful and obtained the Barry Dock and Railway Act of 14th August, 1884. Although the railway they sought through the Rhondda Valley to the Ocean collieries was not authorised, a railway from Barry to the Lower Rhondda to connect with the Taff at Trehafod was permitted, as well as a short branch from that railway to the Taff main line near Treforest. This meant that a large quantity of coal collected by the Taff from the collieries in the Rhondda, Aberdare and Taff valleys would have to be handed over to the Barry at the two junctions, a loss of extensive mileage revenue to the Taff and equally serious loss of revenue to the Trustees at the Bute Docks.

In desperation the old enemies clung together in their hour of peril, and sought ways and means to deal with the situation. It seemed the only possible solution was to unite, and a Bill was promoted in the 1885 Session for such fusion. Terms were agreed for the Taff to either lease, or purchase outright, the Bute Dock undertaking. However, the freighters would have none of it, and their opposition led to clauses being inserted in the Bill which neither the Trustees nor the TVR would accept, hence, reluctantly, they were forced to withdraw the Bill.

On 10th April, 1883 the Trustees made agreement with the TVR for improved access to, and facilities at, the docks. They leased land to the TVR for massive coal storage sidings, gave them the right to convey the traffic direct to the tip sidings at the Roath Dock when completed, offered them land at the dock for erecting locomotive facilities including a turntable near the Roath Basin, and agreed to a more convenient direct connection from the Taff's East Branch to the coal tips on the west side of the East Dock. On 6th August, 1885 the TVR obtained an Act, with the Trustees support, for the construction of their own Roath Dock branch, from a junction from the main line south of Llandaff, skirting the eastern side of Cardiff, and curving back in a south west direction to the dock itself. The Roath Dock opened on 24th August, 1887 and the Taff's Roath Branch was completed and opened 23rd April, 1888.

Following the failure of the TVR/Bute fusion in the 1885 Session, the Marquis decided he could no longer continue to finance the docks from his own resources, hence the Trustees obtained an Act in the 1886 Session to set up a corporate company to take control of the dock undertaking and raise extra capital. This was the Bute Docks (Transfer) Act of 25th June, 1886 by which the Bute Docks Company took over from the Trustees as from 1st January, 1887. The new company started negotiations with the TVR and a further Bill for amalgamation was deposited for the 1888 Session, but once again the opposition proved too powerful for it to become law. A final attempt

was made in the 1889 Session for the Taff to take over the management of the docks, but again it was rejected.

Hence the parties were left to face the imminent opening of Barry
Dock with fear and despondency. In a last desperate bid George
Fisher, the Taff's ageing general manager, who had been with the
company since the day it opened, slashed the coal tariff from
0.71 pence per ton per mile to 0.55 pence, a reduction of about
22½%. But all to no avail as far as the TVR was concerned; directly
Barry Dock opened on 18th July, 1889 it was filled to capacity from the
very first day, exactly as David Davies had predicted. However, as
the table below illustrates, it was the TVR and its Penarth allies that
suffered, the loss to the Bute Co. was negligible in proportion.

Year	Cardiff	Coal shipments from Penarth	Barry
1888	7,604,856	3,390,252	–
1890	7,420,080	1,566,599	3,192,691

Of the Barry's total no less than 2,831,537 tons were handed over to
them by the TVR at Trehafod and Treforest Junctions.

Hence, whilst the Bute Docks suffered little loss, mainly due to the
still expanding steam coal export trade, the Taff lost mileage revenue
on nearly 3m tons of coal, whilst the Penarth Co. had their coal
shipments halved. The Taff shareholders were furious, heads had to
roll and roll they did. In 1891, after a committee of enquiry, the entire
Board of Directors were replaced and most of the senior officers
sacked. The only good result from the Taff's point of view was that
Mr Ammon Beasley, an assistant at Paddington GWR, was appointed
general manager, a very wise choice of an outstandingly successful
manager, and he gradually steered the Taff through the crisis and
into another period of modest prosperity.

As far as the Bute Co. was concerned, coal exports were maintained
at an average of about 7½m tons for the next few years, hence they
saw no further need to continue wooing the TVR. With the expanding coal trade even the exports at Barry and Penarth left plenty for the
Bute Docks, and the TVR had no alternative but to ship the bulk of
their traffic at Cardiff. Late in 1893 they felt secure enough to promote
a Bill for a fourth major dock and, by the Bute Dock Act of 31st July,
1894, obtained authorisation to construct the Queen Alexandra dock,
by far the largest at Cardiff, although they waited for the trade to
further develop before commencing construction, and the dock was
not opened until 13th July, 1907. Initially it had been intended to
name this dock the South Dock, but in view of the acceptance by HM
King Edward VII of the invitation to perform the opening ceremony,
the name was changed to that of his Queen.

The first USA S160 class 2–8–0 (No. 1609) to arrive in this country being off-loaded at the Queen Alexandra Dock, 27th November, 1942. *British Rail*

Former RR 0–6–0T No. 604 (RR 32) moves a line of USA 0–6–0Ts along the quayside after unloading from the S.S. *Lakehurst*, Queen Alexandra Dock, December 1943. *British Rail*

A line of ten USA 0–4–4–0 Whitcomb diesels near Roath Storage Sidings, after unloading at the Queen Alexandra Dock, December 1943. The locos are awaiting movement to the USA Transportation Depot located at the repair shop at Newport Ebbw Jn loco shed. *British Rail*

Loading two Sir Lindsay Parkinson locos, bound for Alexandria on the S.S. *Clan McMurray*, using a USA floating crane *General Ike*, Queen Alexandra Dock, May 1945. The two locos, *Montevideo* HC 1683/1937 (being lifted) and *Nellie* HC 1698/1938 were shipped to work on a contract in Egypt.

Associated British Ports (South Wales Group)

[60 & 61 Vict.] *Cardiff Railway Act, 1897.* [Ch. ccvii.]

CHAPTER ccvii.

An Act for empowering the Bute Docks Company to construct certain Railways for conferring upon that Company certain running powers for empowering them to construct a Low Water Pier for changing the name of the Company and for authorising the Company to raise Additional Capital and for other purposes..

A.D. 1897.

[6th August 1897.]

WHEREAS under the Bute Docks (Transfer) Act 1886 the Bute Docks Company (in this Act called "the Company") were incorporated and became the owners of the Bute Docks at Cardiff :

49 & 50 Vict c. lxxxvi.

And whereas improved railway access from the docks of the Company to the Taff and Rhondda Valleys and other portions of the Glamorganshire coalfield is an object of local and public importance :

And whereas in furtherance of that object it is expedient to authorise the Company to construct the railways in this Act described :

And whereas in connexion with the construction of such railways it is expedient to confer on the Company certain running powers :

And whereas it is expedient to authorise the Company to construct the low water pier described in this Act :

And whereas it is expedient that the name of the Company be changed :

And whereas it is expedient to authorise the Company to raise further capital and to make such other provisions as this Act contains :

And whereas John Patrick Crichton Stuart the present Marquess of Bute has surrendered into the hands of the Company five thousand ordinary shares standing in his name being part of the fully paid ordinary shares allotted to him under the provisions

[*Price 3s. 6d.*]

The first page of the 1897 Act that changed the name of the company to the Cardiff Railway Company.

However, long before such happening the Bute Co. sought to oppose the Taff directly, by presenting a Bill in the 1895 Session to promote direct railways into the valleys in competition to the TVR, but this does not form part of the history of the docks, and the continuing feud with the Bute Co. and its successors the Cardiff Railway Co. is told in the second section of this book.

The company changed its name to the Cardiff Railway by virtue of Section 60 of their Act of 6th August, 1897 which, it was hoped, would alter their status to that of a dock owning railway company on similar lines to the Barry. In the event, as told elsewhere, the railway turned out to be a white elephant, and the docks continued to be the main undertaking of the Company.

Despite the changes from the Trusteeship to the Bute Dock Co. and then to the railway company, the current holder of the title Marquis of Bute was still the mainstay of the concern, and the principal shareholder. In the Cardiff area, and indeed elsewhere, it was always looked upon as the Marquis' docks or railway as the case may be, and it was still largely the Marquis' capital that financed all major construction. In 1891 the Dowlais Co. erected a massive steel works on the moors immediately east of the Bute Docks, and the Marquis personally financed the necessary sidings and connections to the dock lines, and these were extended as further works sprang up in the same area. These lines, although worked as part of the Cardiff Railway's dock sidings, always remained the property of the Marquis himself, until finally sold to the GWR following the amalgamation of the Cardiff Railway into the GWR group in 1922. The Marquis also had to dig very deeply into his own pocket in respect of the construction of both the Queen Alexandra Dock and the railway into the Taff valley. In connection with the Fusion Bills of 1909 (see railway section) it was reported that of the £2,762,000 then outlayed on the two projects, the Marquis had spent £2m. It was also reported that the capital of the company at that time was £6,333,300 of which the Marquis and his family held £3,839,543 in shares.

By 1909 the Taff's percentage of the traffic at Cardiff Docks was diminishing. It still provided 52 per cent of the traffic, compared with 75 per cent in 1882. Comparative figures for the other principal railways using the docks were RR, 29 per cent (17 per cent in 1882) and GWR, 18 per cent (7½ per cent).

The visit paid by King Edward VII in 1907 to open the Queen Alexandra Dock was followed, five years later, by a further royal visit when King George V and Queen Mary started and concluded a tour of Dowlais and the Taff, Rhondda and Aberdare valleys on Thursday 27th June, 1912, from the Royal Yacht berthed at the Queen Alexandra Dock.

This tour was undertaken by rail transport, the TVR making up a royal train comprising their Directors' saloon, a composite carriage and a passenger brake van (all three vehicles having been constructed at the Taff's carriage works at Cathays, Cardiff), and was a triumph of organisation by the CR, RR, TVR and GWR, all of whose lines were used at some stage of the tour.

The King and Queen boarded the Taff "royal train" at the quayside, and a Cardiff Railway locomotive hauled it through the dock sidings to Crockherbtown Jn, where TVR 4-4-2T No. 173 was waiting to take over. Unfortunately the number of the Cardiff locomotive was not given in the reports, but it would seem probable that it was one of the vacuum fitted 0-6-0STs purchased second hand from the GWR.

A couple of years earlier enthusiastic crowds had given a rousing send off to Captain Scott and his team as they departed from the Bute East Dock on his ill fated expedition to the South Pole. His vessel, a converted whaling ship, the *Terra Nova*, had put into the Bute Docks to take on best Welsh steam coal, and passed out from the East Dock to the entrance channel on 15th June, 1910.

The export coal trade reached its peak in 1913 when no less than 10½m tons were shipped at the Bute Docks. Other exports amounted to a further 1m tons and imports to over 2m tons, giving a total tonnage dealt with at the port of 13,676,941 tons. Such tonnages were never to be achieved again, the dislocation caused by World War I having a serious effect on the coal trade, including the permanent loss of some markets. During 1918 the total tonnage dealt with at Cardiff was only 8¼m tons, the export coal trade having slumped to 6m tons.

The expected post war trade revival was quickly shattered by a lengthy miner's strike in 1921 which plunged coal exports to less than 4m tons, and the same year Parliament passed its Grouping of Railways Act. The Cardiff Docks and the railways feeding them were, in common with most of the other docks and railways in South Wales, amalgamated within the Great Western Railway Group. Thus at last, after years of frustration, legislation, litigation and recrimination, the dream of a combined railway and dock enterprise at Cardiff had been realised, but not quite as the local promoters had intended. Despite their numerous differences, they were united in the view that overall control should be based at Cardiff. Whilst all had great respect for the GWR and its reputation, there were many fears expressed as to the wisdom of control of the docks passing far away from the scene of activity, to Paddington.

However, the GWR were fully aware of the immense dock undertakings they now controlled in South Wales, and quickly located the office of their Chief Docks Manager at Cardiff, actually in the former

Cardiff Railways head office, in the heart of the dockland. Further the GWR recognised the long and outstanding contribution which the successive Marquises of Bute had made both to the development of the docks, and to the city itself, and decreed that the docks at Cardiff would always be known as the Bute Docks.

Before proceeding to the later history of the docks, a brief outline of the undertaking as at 1922 should be given. The Bute Docks, undoubtedly one of the world's largest coal ports, ranked third in the list of British ports for the total tonnage handled. The undertaking comprised of four main docks, the Bute West and Bute East, the Roath and the Queen Alexandra, plus the Roath Basin – virtually a further small dock in its own right. The combined area of deep water was no less than 165 acres and the length of quayage 35,640 feet (6¾ miles). Whilst all the docks were well equipped for coal exporting, the north quays at the two modern docks (the Roath and Queen Alexandra) were reserved and equipped for the general cargo trade.

There were 59 coal shipping appliances (28 fixed, 13 movable and 18 patent Lewis Hunter coaling cranes), the general cargo quays provided with ample cranage, transit sheds and warehouses, flour mills, granaries, cattle lairs and cold stores, and there were twelve graving and floating docks for ship repairs. The 25 warehouses had a combined floor area of almost one million square feet, whilst the two cold stores had a combined storage capacity of 425,000 cubic feet. Apart from this impressive list of dock equipment and storage facilities, many of the large firms trading at the port had private warehouses and mechanical handling equipment. The main export trade other than coal was steel rails, ironwork, patent fuel and general cargo, whilst the chief imports were iron ore, timber, pitwood, grain, flour, cattle and frozen meat.

Improved trade figures for the year 1923, when over 8½m tons of coal were shipped from the Bute docks, gave the impetus to the GWR to spend further capital on the coal shipping facilities. Several hoists were extensively overhauled, or renewed, a large number of storage sidings added, the docks telephone network was greatly improved and the installation of modern hydraulic pumping stations undertaken. The following year the GWR introduced (initially at Port Talbot) 20 ton coal wagons, which gave a quicker turn round at the docks and required less storage siding capacity. Colliery owners were induced to use such wagons by a reduction in both railway and dock charges for corresponding loads using the new wagons.

However, the short post war boom in the coal trade passed all too quickly, and by 1925 the loss of certain foreign markets due to war reparations, coupled with the increasing use of the internal combustion engine, meant the demand for steam coal had started its inevitable and final decline. The general strike of 1926 further aggravated matters, and that was soon followed by the years of depression that preceded World War II. By 1933 coal exports had declined to just over 4½m tons, but this total was maintained, and slightly exceeded, over the years until 1939. In order to effect economies certain pooling arrangements were made between the GWR and LMSR. These were introduced on 1st January, 1933, one result being that the LMS (former LNWR) working to Cardiff Docks was discontinued, traffic to/from that railway being diverted over the GWR main lines via Newport and Hereford. Due to Messrs Guest Keen & Co.'s decision to modernise its East Moors Steel Works, completed in 1935, general cargo trading figures were maintained in the pre-World War II years. The works, sited alongside the docks, required a high level of iron ore importation, and this was coupled with a correspondingly high level of finished steel export.

The dislocation to normal trading brought about by the 1939–45 War saw the steam coal export trade reduced to insignificant totals, when compared with the boom years before World War I. During 1940 it dropped to 3¼m tons, but by 1945 it had slumped to a mere 1m tons. Against that the Bute Docks made a major contribution to the War effort, with military traffic and troops keeping it working flat out. Amongst the many military uses was the loading and unloading of various locomotives. The first, as far as is known, to have been despatched from Cardiff, was 2–8–0 Stanier '8F' W.D. No. 361, loaded for Egypt in June 1941, followed three months later by 22 more of the same class for Persia, Nos. 301/3/5–8/13/20/8/30/1/5/7/69/72/88/9, 401/3/8/12/3.

The following year saw the first of a flood of specially built American 2–8–0s (S160 class) when Nos. 1604/7/9/24 were discharged on 27th November, 1942. The initial batches of these engines were for assisting the hard pressed railways of Britain and most of those unloaded at Cardiff were sent to Swindon for GWR use. Those unloaded from September 1943 onwards were for USA Army use, and were sent to Ebbw Jn (Newport) where the US Transportation Corps set up HQ for the testing and then storage, of the engines in readiness for the Allied invasion of Europe. Many of these USA 2–8–0s reached Cardiff in large vessels known as "Sea Trains" which had three decks with rail tracks accommodating the locos on their long and perilous voyage from the United States.

The 2–8–0s were followed, in December 1943, by a number of USA 0–6–0T shunting engines, also some 0–4–4–0 main line diesel electric locos, the latter painted sand colour. Some of the 0–6–0Ts

British Austerity 2–8–0s awaiting shipment on the quayside at the Queen
Alexandra Dock, Summer 1945. *British Rail*

The Hawker Siddeley prototype 4000 hp diesel electric locomotive *Kestrel*
being lifted by the floating crane at the Queen Alexandra Dock, June 1971, for
loading aboard the Russian vessel *Kpachokamck* (*left*) *en route* to the USSR.
Leslie W. Hansen (Courtesy Welsh Industrial and Maritime Museum, Cardiff)

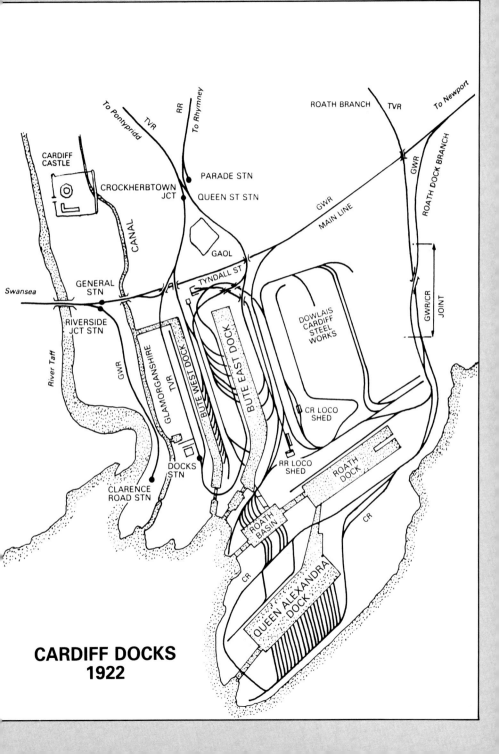

CARDIFF DOCKS
1922

were used for a short while by local sheds (Cardiff East Dock, New-port Pill, Barry etc.), but were soon put to store as well. As GWR footplate men were not familiar with the diesels, these were only used on rare occasions on the main line for experimental purposes, although they did run light engine on trial trips. The last American engines (2–8–0s) to arrive were only received a week or two before the invasion of Europe, 6th June 1944.

These war time engines were by no means the first to be dealt with at the Bute Docks, but were certainly the first to be handled in large numbers. The occasional engine had been shipped from early days, but undoubtedly the most famous was the pride and joy of the GWR, 4–6–0 No. 6000 *King George V*, which, accompanied by the replica broad gauge locomotive *North Star*, started on her triumphant visit to America by being loaded – in three sections, boiler, frame/wheels and tender – onto a comparatively small vessel, the *Chicago Star*, at the Roath Dock on 3rd August, 1927. Another famous engine to pass through the docks was LMS Pacific No. 6220 *Coronation* (actually No. 6229 renamed/renumbered) which was unloaded on its return from America on 16th February, 1942. This engine had also been on exhibi-tion in the States, but was stranded there on the outbreak of war, and had to await a "convenient" time to return.

Towards the end of the war, and in the very early post war period, an even larger number of engines were shipped from Cardiff to back up the forces who had landed and were consolidating their foothold on the continent. However, it was after the re-capture of the port of Cherbourg that the engines left Cardiff in quantity. First to go were 183 of the American 2–8–0s, part of the three batches stored locally, the others being shipped from Southampton. These were quickly followed by some of the earlier engines that had been working on the GWR and LNER. That was mainly in September 1944. In the next few months further 2–8–0 tender engines were despatched from Cardiff Docks, these were LMS Stanier class 8s, and the Riddles Austerity type. During those hectic few months it was recorded that 565 engines were shipped from the Bute Docks.

Peacetime conditions saw the steam coal export trade continue to dwindle, although 1947 and 1951 were the only years before 1955 when the total dipped below the 1m mark but after that the figures were insignificant as the trade slowly died away. The railways, along with their docks, were nationalised as from 1st January, 1948, and great efforts were made to find alternative traffic. However, Cardiff, along with the other South Wales ports, had been planned principally for the coal trade and, with much of the quayside laid with tip roads, the efforts met with only partial success.

A complete transformation was required but this did not come about until 1963 following the creation of the British Transport Docks Board, when revolutionary decisions were made. At that time the miles of coal sidings were still *in situ* despite their low usage, and few of the remaining coal tips were needed. The bold decision was made to cease the export of coal from Cardiff Docks, and that took effect from August 1964.

The old West Dock of 1839 was closed entirely as from 31st January, 1964, although it had ceased to be involved in the coal trade for many years, and the rail connection from the former TVR's East Branch had been taken out about 1953. The West Dock was filled in about 1970. On the 20th December, 1964 the former Rhymney Railway's branch to the docks was taken out of use and, with the closure of the TVR's Roath Dock branch as from 6th May, 1968, the last direct rail communication between the valley railways and Cardiff Docks ceased to exist. Henceforth rail traffic to/from the docks used the two former GWR routes via Long Dyke or Pengam Junctions, and even the former was taken out of use as from 12th June, 1978. Between these closures the East Dock had been taken out of commercial use on 31st January, 1970.

However, these changes enabled the port to be transformed, and made it possible to secure new markets. Removal of some 305 acres of tips sidings provided ample quayage for the provision of modern cargo facilities. A freightliner terminal was put in at Pengam close to the remaining junction to the docks, whilst modern roads connect the docks to the national road network. Specialised berths have been provided for cargoes such as packaged timber, fruit and refined petroleum products. A modern timber terminal able to cater for bulk timber carrying vessels has been constructed. The two docks that remain (the Roath and the Queen Alexandra) are worked as one with the connecting channel, the lock for the QA dock now serving as the entrance to both docks. This lock is 850 feet long and 90 feet wide, and vessels up to 32,000 tons can enter port. The water depth is 36 ft in the Roath dock and 37 ft in the QA dock.

The total trade at the dock rose to 4m tons in 1973, whereas in 1959 it reached only 2¼m tons. From 1965 onwards and in the 1970s the port achieved an annual financial operating surplus which, for the period 1971 to 1976 inclusive, amounted to between 6 and 8 per cent on the Capital Value, a far cry from the 3 per cent which was all that the Cardiff Railway Company yielded at the height of the coal boom. A dark shadow was cast on the new prosperity by the loss of iron ore and steel trade which followed the closure of East Moors Steel Works on 28th April, 1978. However, a new Rod Mill was built on the site a couple of years later, and this has brought some trade to road, rail and docks. Scrap metal is brought into Messrs Birds by road, there it is crushed and despatched to the Tremorfa Works (just west of the docks boundary) by rail. At the Tremorfa Works billets are made which are sent by rail across to the Castle Rod Mill, and the finished products are mostly despatched in rail wagons to the quayside for loading.

The main trade at present (December 1985) is:

Imports – Timber from Scandinavia, Malaya, Russia, North America
Fruit from Israel, New Zealand and South Africa
Dairy Products from New Zealand
Oil (occasional) taken from docks in short wheelbase rail tankers
Exports – Grain to Russia and other countries
Scrap metal to Italy, Greece, the Far East and South America
Wire and Steel Products to various countries
Small coal to the Continent

Although the West Dock has been filled in, the old Basin now forms a "dry dock" as part of the Industrial and Maritime Museum which was set up alongside, and opened on 15th April, 1977. The East Dock still contains water and at one stage speedboat racing was held there and it was hoped it would become a centre for the sport. However, certain difficulties could not be overcome, and in October 1978 it was announced that the old dock would be transformed into a boating lake, but nothing came of that either, and the northern section of the former West Dock and the East Dock became somewhat derelict and untidy.

Such was the case until Associated British Ports took over as from the end of 1982. Plans were drawn up to develop the site, and work has just commenced (November 1985) on the South Cardiff "Redevelopment Plan" which incorporates the old West and East Dock area, and the land between. When completed a network of roads will connect with both the city and by-passes, and the main feature will be new South Glamorgan County Offices. This is towards the southern end of the site, and adjacent to a proposed superstore complex. At the northern end there are plans for a Technology Campus, with housing for students alongside. Between the two main centres outlined would be land for 720 houses, all the above being to the west side of the East Dock. It is proposed to keep water in the dock, and there stable a paddle steamer as a leisure cum dancing complex, whilst near the southern end of the dock a site has been reserved for a National Theatre.

If the complete scheme comes into fruition it will revitalise the area, and should give a new lease of life to Bute Road railway station, which is now only used for peak period passenger traffic, as the station is but a short distance from the new County Offices and superstore. The development area would become an essential part of modern Cardiff, as exactly the same area was responsible for the growth of Cardiff from insignificance to a great seaport over a century and a quarter ago.

The principal export at the docks was steam coal. Here S.S. *Martita* is taking coal from four traverser hoists at the Queen Alexandra Dock at an unknown date.   *Author's Collection*

PROPRIETORS:

THE CARDIFF RAILWAY COMPANY.

CHAIRMAN:

THE MARQUESS OF BUTE, K.T

GENERAL MANAGER:

SIR WILLIAM THOMAS LEWIS BART

SUPERINTENDENT:

JAMES HURMAN

———————+ⁱ₀ⁱ+———————

NOTICE.

The CARDIFF RAILWAY Co. will not be responsible for any loss or damage arising from stoppage of work or delay consequent upon partial or general strikes, lockouts, or combination of or by any persons whether or not in the Company's employment or service, or from any operation of nature, the Queen's enemies, fire, riot, accident, wilful or other damage, or otherwise.

WILLIAM THOMAS LEWIS,
General Manager.

JUNE, 1899.

Title page from the Cardiff Railway official handbook of the Bute Docks, June 1899.

Part Two

The Cardiff Railway

In November 1895 the two opposing companies promoted Bills (see Docks section p. 32) aimed at cutting out, as far as possible, the dependence each had on the other. The Bute Co. sought powers to change its status to that of a dock owning railway company, promoting railways in direct competition with the Taff, whilst the latter sought powers, in the guise of an independent company, to construct a major dock to compete with the Bute.

In 1885 the Marquis had purchased the Glamorganshire Canal, which the Bute Co. proposed to acquire, along with the Aberdare Canal, close both and convert them to railways. This would have given them a main line to Merthyr and a branch through the Aberdare coalfield. The Bill proposed no less than 21 different railways, mostly short branches from the two principal railways to collieries and factories, but also included a junction with the TVR south of Pontypridd, to divert coal from the Rhondda valleys to its own route to the docks. In addition a further railway from the docks to southern Monmouthshire was proposed. This would have headed eastwards from the docks, passed over the South Wales main line on the approaches to Newport, and headed northwards to connect with the GWR's Western Valley branch south of Bassaleg Junction. This railway was designed to attract colliery companies in the Western and Sirhowy valleys to ship their coal at Cardiff in preference to Newport.

The Taff countered by being the backbone behind a Bill seeking powers to construct a large modern dock on the east bank of the River Ely, opposite Penarth Dock, called the Windsor Dock. After their narrow victory in the Lords in 1873 they dared not risk promoting such Bill under their own name, and it went forward as from the landowners – the Windsor family – but surviving records clearly show that the Taff were not only behind the scheme financially, but that the whole matter, the Bill itself, estimates and plans, were dealt with at the TVR head office in Cardiff. Such dock, if authorised, would have made the Taff virtually independent of the Bute docks, whilst the railways the Bute proposed would have dealt a crippling blow to the TVR. However, as expected, the opposition to both proposals was intense, and both Bills were rejected in the 1896 Session.

Undaunted, the companies renewed battle on very similar lines in the following Session, and on that occasion the Bute Co. had a partial, but most important, success. By its Act of 6th August, 1897 the company's name was changed to the Cardiff Railway Co., and it was given powers to construct five railways totalling 12 m. 3 ch. in length. Of these Railways Nos 1 and 4 were the vital ones, covering a

43

main line commencing by a junction from the Rhymney Railway (Heath Jn 3 m. 16 ch. from the docks terminus) to the Pontypridd area, and a branch connecting with the TVR south of Treforest.

The Act also granted the company running powers over the RR from the docks through Caerphilly and on to Penrhos Jn, where it was hoped to divert some of the coal traffic passing over the Alexandra Dock and Railway to Cardiff. There is no record that the CR ever exercised these powers beyond Heath Jn.

The other railways authorised by the Act were short branches in the Pontypridd area which, on paper, appeared reasonably harmless to TVR interests, but most useful to the Cardiff as a springboard from which to extend further into Taff territory at a later date if Parliament so willed.

The second Windsor Dock scheme was again rejected, leaving the Taff in a serious situation. The Bute interests owned major collieries in the Treherbert area, and were also landowners elsewhere in the colliery belt and nothing was more certain than that a considerable quantity of coal traffic would be diverted to the CR authorised line. This would mean a substantial loss of revenue over the 11½ miles between Treforest (Cardiff) Jn and the docks, vital mileage revenue on which Taff profits depended.

Flushed with success, the CR promoted a further Bill in the 1898 Session to extend northwards into Taff territory, and also construct an independent line from north of the proposed Heath Jn to their docks. Again the Taff backed a third Windsor Dock scheme but Parliament, having reached its decision the previous year, rejected everything except the independent line to the docks. By the CR Act of 12th August, 1898 authorisation was given to construct a railway from Roath Dock; this would have paralleled the TVR's Roath Dock branch to just before that branch passed under the RR, from which point it would have curved northwards, and then westwards to pass under the RR to join the line authorised the previous year. Due to the later successful opposition by the TVR to the CR's proposed junction at Treforest, the independent line to the docks was never constructed, although as a small part of the GWR's Roath Dock branch (authorised 7th August, 1896 and opened 2nd November, 1903) ran over a similar path for 26 chains on the approach to the Roath Dock, that short section was classed as GWR/CR joint line by agreement between the two companies dated 15th November, 1901.

With the third rejection of their more ambitious schemes both companies decided against a fourth encounter. The Cardiff decided to press ahead with the decided advantage they had gained, whilst the Taff concentrated on ways and means to legally obstruct, or at least delay as long as possible, the coupling of the Cardiff line with their

Cardiff Railway 0–6–0ST No. 23 heading the 5.22 pm Cardiff RR to Rhydy-felin railmotor, approaching Heath Jn, 11th October, 1913.

Locomotive Club of Great Britain

The 6.32 pm Coryton to Cardiff Queen Street at Heath Jn. Ex-TVR 'A' class 0–6–2T No. 343 heads a set which includes two conversions from former TVR steam rail cars. 27th July, 1953.

S. Rickard

The new Heath Jn on the opening day, 19th November, 1984. A DMU gingerly descends the 1 in 50 slope to connect with the Coryton branch at Heath (LL). Note the former path of branch (*right*).   British Rail

The original Heath Halt as opened 1911. The 'staggered' up platform is not visible on this photograph.   *Lens of Sutton*

own at Treforest. In 1898 the Cardiff placed Contract No. 1 with Messrs Monk and Newall of Liverpool, for construction of the first 3¾ miles from Heath Jn to Tongwynlais, whilst the same year the Taff purchased a strip of land running along the east side of their railway south of Treforest.

This was alleged to be for the purpose of putting in a down siding, but it conveniently included the portion over which the CR would have to pass to effect the junction. In the event no sidings were ever laid on this strip, but it proved vital in the final legal battle between the two companies.

Whilst Contract 1 was proceeding, the third Marquis of Bute, Chairman of the Cardiff Railway, died on 9th February, 1900. His heir, the fourth Marquis, was then under age, and Lord Edmund Talbot became the new Chairman. On attaining his seniority the Marquis was, on 4th July, 1902, elected to the Cardiff Board and remained so to eventually become the last Chairman of the company on 25th June, 1915.

On 30th January, 1902 the contractors forwarded their certificate of completion of Contract 1, and plans were immediately prepared for the remainder of the line. These were sufficiently advanced for a plan of the proposed junction at Treforest to be sent to the TVR in October. This showed a double line junction with the Taff passenger lines, followed by a double crossover to the mineral lines on the west side.

At this juncture it would be as well to briefly describe the situation that existed at the site. The Taff had four running lines, the pair on the eastern (or CR) side used mainly, but not solely, for passenger traffic, the other pair for mineral and goods traffic. Immediately north of the proposed crossover was the double line junction with the Barry Railway again followed by a crossover this time to the passenger lines. After leaving the Taff the Barry fanned out into exchange sidings on which the Taff placed traffic for Barry docks, and collected empties for the collieries. As trains of coal often came down the Taff with part load for Cardiff and part for Barry, such trains had to be split at the junction, the rear section (for Cardiff) remaining on the down mineral line, whilst the Barry part of the train was taken to the exchange sidings, and the Taff engine returned to its train. As the coal traffic down that Taff section had exceeded 8m tons in 1898, and was increasing annually, and as some of the trains with coal for the CR would have to be dealt with similarly, severe delays to the Taff's own traffic was inevitable. There is no doubt that Parliament had authorised the Cardiff junction at a most inconvenient site from the traffic point of view.

However, the Cardiff's proposal was quickly rejected on three grounds, firstly that the proposed junction and crossover exceeded the limits of deviation shown on the deposited plans, secondly that the CR had no authority to connect with all four lines of the TVR, and finally the short distance between the proposed junction and the crossover involved running powers by the CR over the TVR, powers they did not possess.

The CR expected counter proposals from the Taff, but these were not forthcoming as they felt under no obligation to assist the opposition. In fact both in 1902 and 1903 the TVR put forward Bills proposing that the connection between the two lines should be just north of Taffs Well, several miles further southwards. This would have given them considerable extra mileage revenue on the coal traffic, but would have made the CR north of the connection virtually useless, as little local traffic was expected. Both Bills were rejected in Parliament, leaving the CR to make the next move.

As usual in such disputes an arbitrator was called in, and Mr J.C. Inglis, general manager of the GWR, was appointed in October 1903. The Taff immediately objected to arbitration, advising Mr Inglis that, as the Cardiff proposal exceeded the limits of deviation, he had no authority to make a decision. This caused further delay and eventually the Cardiff decided to abandon arbitration and ask the Courts to establish the legality of the position. Meanwhile, they decided to press on with construction of the northern section of the line and, in December 1904, placed Contract No. 2 with Messrs Thomas Oliver and Sons for completion to the junction at Treforest.

The case in law was settled on 5th June, 1905 when, in the Court of Chancery, Mr Justice Farwell decided that the proposed mode of junction was not lawful in accordance with the authorisation of the 1897 Act. He judged that a junction was a fixed point and that no railway company could wobble it about to suit their own convenience. Initially the CR intended to appeal, but decided that the best course of action was to go back to Parliament for an Act which would clearly define both the mode and point of junction. This resulted in their Act of 4th August, 1906 which authorised a junction with all four lines of the TVR, and gave the company powers to lease, but not purchase, the necessary section of the strip of land which the Taff had purchased in 1898 over which the CR had to pass to get to the junction. The 1897 Act had decreed that transfer of traffic should not involve any shunting on the Taff main line, and in the 1906 Act the CR had this clarified in that parting a train on the main line, for one section to proceed to the Cardiff line, did not constitute shunting. With this Act the CR felt home and dry at last, but the TVR had put forward sufficient argument for a clause to be inserted that the

Heath Halt (LL) as enlarged by the GWR. A down auto, powered by an 0–6–0PT, about to leave for Cardiff Queen Street; 14th February, 1948.

Ian Wright

Heath (LL) seen on 19th April, 1986. After the 1966 singling of the branch, the down platform was retained.

Bob Pugh

A down train consisting of CR 0–6–0T No. 7 and two trailers approaches
Heath Halt on 17th May, 1919.   *Locomotive Club of Great Britain*

Birchgrove Halt, 25th May, 1958. 0–6–2T No. 6614 running in on a five coach
suburban train from Coryton.   *Michael Hale*

The Cardiff Railway Company.

BOARD OF DIRECTORS.

The MARQUIS OF BUTE, Rothesay, Bute, N.B. (*Chairman*).
A. R. C. PITMAN, 48, Castle Street, Edinburgh (*Deputy-Chairman*).
The LORD MERTHYR, Hean Castle, Saundersfoot, Pem.
F. I. PITMAN, 14, Austin Friars, London, E.C.
The LORD GLANELY, Lacham, Lacock, Wilts.

OFFICERS.

General Manager and Dockmaster -	ERNEST A. PROSSER, C.B.E., Bute Docks, Cardiff.
Assistant General Manager -	C. S. PAGE, Bute Docks, Cardiff.
Secretary - - - -	H. A. ROBERTS, 22a, Queen Anne's Gate, Westminister, S.W.1.
Solicitor - - -	W. LEWIS HARRIS, Castle Street, Cardiff.
Chief Engineer - -	ALARIC HOPE, Bute Docks, Cardiff.
Accountant - - -	J. C. DORE, Bute Docks, Cardiff.
Goods and Warehouse Department	W. N. THOMPSON, M.B.E., Bute Docks, Cardiff.
Deputy-Dockmaster - -	CAPT. W. E. PRITCHARD, Bute Docks, Cardiff.
Collector of Dues - -	W. H. TREATT, Bute Docks, Cardiff.
Mineral and Traffic Manager -	W. J. HOLLOWAY, Bute Docks, Cardiff.
Stores Superintendent -	J. S. KENDALL, Bute Docks, Cardiff.

TELEGRAPHIC ADDRESSES AND TELEPHONE NUMBERS.

General Manager - -	"Endeavour," Cardiff. 1421 (6 Lines), Cardiff.
General Manager's London Office -	"Prosser," c/o Tydfil, Vic. London. 1713 Victoria.
Secretary - - -	"Roberts," c/o Tydfil, Vic. London. 1713 Victoria.
Engineer - - -	"Resident," Cardiff.
Collector of Dues - -	"Collector," c/o "Endeavour," Cardiff
Goods and Warehouse Department -	"Storage," Cardiff.
Mineral and Traffic Department -	"Traffic.," Cardiff.
Deputy-Dockmaster - -	"Dockmaster," Cardiff.
Stores Superintendent -	"Stores," c/o "Endeavour," Cardiff

1421 (6 Lines), Cardiff.

From the official handbook "Cardiff (Bute Docks) as a Shipping Port". Cardiff Railway c.1919

junction was not to be opened for traffic until the Cardiff had provided exchange sidings of sufficient length and extent to accommodate the traffic. The Act also allowed a minor diversion, 19 chains in length, in the Cardiff main line approaching the junction, to enable the junction with the four lines of the Taff to be effected with a curve of not less than ten chains radius.

With such Act the Cardiff felt confident of success and in 1907 completed the formation, and all heavy engineering works, into the field approaching the TVR. Their architects had lost no time in submitting a plan, of the proposed four road junction, to both the TVR and Barry Railway on 6th August, 1906 (only two days after the Act had received the Royal Assent), but to their dismay both companies intimated they were again in dispute. The formal replies dated 11th October, 1906 (TVR) and 25th October, 1906 (Barry) were couched in similar words, i.e. that the proposed junction was not in accordance with the provisions of the 1897 and 1906 Acts.

As before the CR applied for an arbitrator to settle the issue, and again both TVR and Barry objected to arbitration, but on this occasion were over-ruled, and on 12th December, 1906 Mr Inglis was again nominated by the Institute of Civil Engineers. Even so on 31st December, 1906 both companies sent personal letters to Mr Inglis saying that they would consider applying for an injunction to restrain him from proceeding with arbitration. This caused a lengthy delay, but in August 1907 the CR persuaded Mr Inglis to proceed. On receipt of letters to this effect both the Taff and Barry requested postponement of the proceedings as many of their officials were about to go on holiday, and it was not until Thursday 5th December, 1907 that arbitration commenced. Counsel for the CR referred to the Taff's policy of masterly objection, to which the Taff's counsel retorted that "it cannot be masterly unless it is successful, and you cannot be successful unless you are right". He also stated that the junction issue could not be settled without the associated exchange sidings, and suggested arbitration be adjourned until the CR provided plans of such sidings, intimating that once the plan was provided the respective Engineers could get together and resolve matters without further arbitration.

There was no delay by the CR. On 23rd December, 1907 a plan of the proposed exchange sidings was sent to the TVR who, as usual, objected. The resumed arbitration started on 20th February, 1908 and it was only six days earlier that the Taff passed their formal objection to the latest plan. They made no direct criticism, but merely suggested that the mode of junction should revert to the 1902 plan, which had already been declared illegal by the Court of Chancery! At the arbitration hearing the Taff objected to everything possible. They stated that a direct four line junction would seriously hold up traffic on their main line, that such junction would entail 12 diamond crossings and bring in an element of danger of derailment to their own traffic, and also that the CR exchange sidings were of insufficient length to accommodate a 55 wagon train with engine and van. They claimed that the Cardiff, as a two road railway, had no right to cross the strip of land they had purchased, as such would delay traffic on the siding they proposed putting on the strip (after ten years no attempt had been made to lay such siding, nor was it ever laid). They produced traffic statistics which revealed that for the 24 hours ending 21st November, 1907 no less than 294 trains (76 passengers and 218 goods/mineral) had passed the site and, of these, 121 trains had passed during the peak period from 10.00 am to 6.00 pm, an average of one train every four minutes. One witness said that a check taken between 10.00 am and 8.00 pm revealed that the section had only been clear of trains for a total of 34 minutes. During 1907 a total of 11,190,000 tons of minerals had passed over the section along with an estimated 3½m passengers.

In reply to the objection of insufficient length of the exchange sidings, which were limited to the distance between the north end of the viaduct over the River Taff and the proposed junction, the Cardiff claimed that most of the ten sidings would accommodate a full train, whereas the Taff claimed that they must have measured wagons tight buffered, and had not allowed for loose coupling. Finally the Taff stated that the 17 ft per wagon, on which the Cardiff had based, was not in accordance with the latest RCH specification, nor did it allow for future wagon design. They even had the impudence to suggest that the viaduct over the River Taff should be widened to take ten sidings as well as the main line, to enable the sidings to be extended southwards, retorting that the prohibitive cost was nothing to do with them. The Barry counsel said that, from their point of view, the proposal junction was sited in the worst place it possibly could be on the entire Taff Vale line, and suggested it should be put in further south and well clear of their own junction with the Taff. He said that any train split for the Cardiff Railway would not only foul the Barry Co.'s junction, but cause delays northwards, particularly at Pontypridd just over a mile away.

To a large extent, however, Mr Inglis was tied by the 1906 Act and its associated deposited plan, and issued his award in May 1908 in the form of a drawing (not included in the documents studied) which was generally in accordance with the CR proposals. From that company's point of view the final obstacle had been overcome, but the Taff had other ideas. They knew the CR were in some financial difficulty. More than £2m had been spent on the new Queen Alexandra dock,

Above. The title page of an official report outlining the pro-

Left. From the Welsh Coal and Shipping Handbook of 1919.

A three car DMU arrives at Birchgrove from Coryton on 19th April, 1986.
Bob Pugh

Rhiwbina Halt as seen from the front passenger seat of a down DMU, 7th
August, 1958.
S. Rickard

A more complete view of Rhiwbina after singling, seen on 17th April, 1986. A DMU set from Coryton is running in. *Bob Pugh*

Whitchurch Station looking east in March 1956, showing goods shed on right. At that date the station was virtually as in CR days. *Derek Chaplin*

Whitchurch from the west today, just another stop on the Coryton branch; 19th April, 1986. *Bob Pugh*

Coryton Halt in 1954 looking north to the end of the branch. The run around loop on the left seems already to be out of use. *Stan Cowles*

and a further £¾m on the railway. They owed some £1½m to their bankers, plus nearly £1m to the Marquis who had dug deeply into his own purse to provide ready cash for both schemes. Hence behind the scenes the TVR started negotiations with the CR Board with a view to acquiring their entire undertaking, docks and railway. For many years the Rhymney Railway had also made known their willingness to sell their concern at the right price, hence, as the other principal user of the docks, negotiations took place with them also. The GWR were also contacted and, although not interested in acquiring dock property, were quite agreeable to the Taff taking over, and were prepared to cease running into the dock area and deliver/collect their traffic on exchange sidings to be laid at Pengam (eastern outskirts of Cardiff) adjacent to their main South Wales line.

Negotiations between the parties were successfully concluded in time for two separate Bills (TVR (CR) Vesting and TVR (RR) Vesting) to be presented in November 1908 for the 1909 Session. Details of the agreements reached were made public and, apart from the financial issues, included:

a) The TVR would complete, at their own expense, a temporary junction with the CR at Treforest, and run that line as part of their own system. Coal traffic worked over the Cardiff line would be charged the same as if run over the TVR to the docks. Some of the passenger trains from the heads of the valleys to Cardiff would be routed via the CR line, also a local passenger service would be started between Pontypridd TVR and Cardiff GWR via the Cardiff route. If the fusion Bill failed the CR would be responsible for the cost of laying and removal of the temporary junction.

b) The RR station at Cardiff would be demolished, and the Taff's Queen Street Station enlarged and widened to take TVR, RR and CR trains.

c) The Taff goods shed at Queen St would be demolished and the RR goods shed at nearby Adam St used by both railways.

d) CR and RR employees would be admitted to the Taff's non contributory pension scheme, their prior lengths of service to count as if served on the TVR.

In connection with clauses a) to c) most readers will be surprised to know that such proposals were planned by the local companies some twenty years before they were actually put into effect by the GWR following the 1922 amalgamations.

Although not included in the agreement the Taff stated that they would probably close their hemmed-in locomotive works at West Yard, Cardiff, and enlarge the Rhymney works at Caerphilly and, if so, a works train would be put on from Cardiff to Caerphilly and back for the convenience of the men transferred. (Another proposal fully effected by the GWR in 1926.)

The agreement met with general approval in the Cardiff area, as both the travelling public and railway servants would benefit, neither the RR or CR having pension schemes for their manual staff. Hence the two Bills – the TVR (CR Fusion) and the TVR (RR Fusion) – were promoted with extreme confidence but, behind the scenes, the interests at Barry and Newport, where combined railway/dock enterprise already existed, were uniting to oppose the fusions. There was also opposition from a few colliery companies, as it was feared the amalgamations might cut-out the competitive coal carrying rates that then existed.

The early evidence on the Bills was heard before a House of Lords committee in May 1909, and in order to demonstrate the new unity between the Taff and the Cardiff a double line junction (9 m. 28 ch. (CR) and 11 m. 62 ch. (TVR)) was put in by the Taff to their passenger lines, over which a ceremonial coal train passed on 15th May, 1909. In order to cross the previously disputed strip of TVR land, a low timber trestle bridge was erected. The train comprised twelve wagons of coal from the Bute Colliery at Treherbert, a saloon carriage being attached behind the brake van at the rear to convey the distinguished party, which comprised the Marquis, Directors from both companies, and several leading officials. At Treforest station the train stopped to pick up Mr Ammon Beasley, the TVR general manager, and the Marquis took the opportunity to leave the comfort of the saloon to ride on the locomotive's footplate over the new railway. The local newspaper reported "The Marquis rode on his own engine to open up his new line, with a train of coal from his own colliery, loaded in his own wagons, for shipment at his own docks". (Actually the train engine was TVR '04' class 0–6–2T No. 98, decorated for the occasion at Coke Ovens shed, as was another class '04', No. 102, the latter probably used as a pilot engine which preceded the special train over the new line whilst the carriage was the TVR Directors' saloon.) However, this display of unity evidently impressed their Lordships, as the preamble of the Bills were passed on 28th May.

The jubilation in Cardiff was short lived. The Barry/Newport opposition presented powerful arguments against the Taff–Bute fusion before the Commons' committee, which led to the Bill's rejection on 26th August. With their main Bill lost, the TVR withdrew the Rhymney Railway Fusion Bill. At the Taff Board meeting held on 12th October, the Directors instructed their Engineer to remove the temporary junction and, as events proved, it was never re-instated. There has been speculation as to whether any traffic passed over the junction after the ceremonial train, but this is discounted for two reasons.

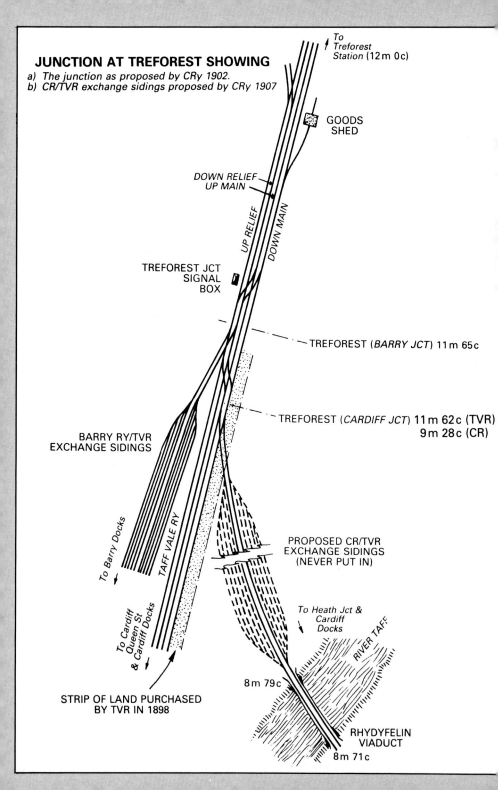

JUNCTION AT TREFOREST SHOWING

a) *The junction as proposed by CRy 1902.*
b) *CR/TVR exchange sidings proposed by CRy 1907*

To
Treforest
Station (12 m 0 c)

GOODS
SHED

*DOWN RELIEF
UP MAIN*

UP RELIEF

DOWN MAIN

TREFOREST JCT
SIGNAL
BOX

— TREFOREST (*BARRY JCT*) 11 m 65 c

— TREFOREST (*CARDIFF JCT*) 11 m 62 c (TVR)
9 m 28 c (CR)

BARRY RY/TVR
EXCHANGE SIDINGS

To Barry Docks

TAFF VALE RY

PROPOSED CR/TVR
EXCHANGE SIDINGS
(NEVER PUT IN)

To Heath Jct &
Cardiff
Docks

RIVER TAFF

To Cardiff
Queen St
& Cardiff Docks

8 m 79 c

STRIP OF LAND PURCHASED
BY TVR IN 1898

RHYDYFELIN
VIADUCT

8 m 71 c

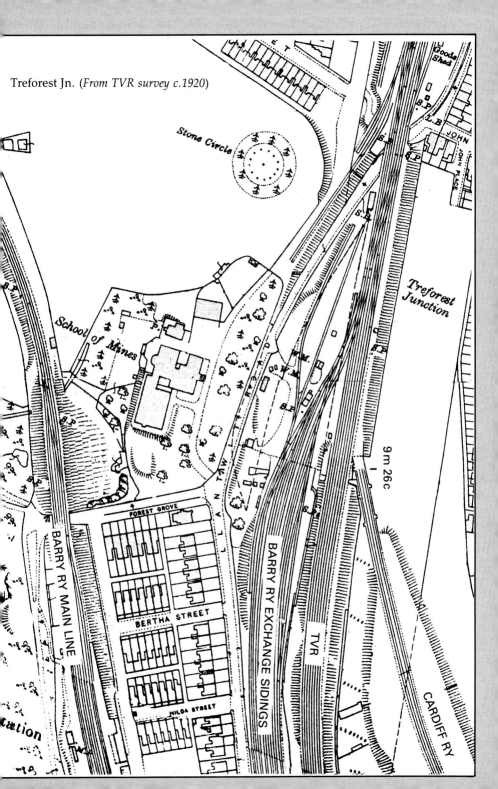

Treforest Jn. (*From TVR survey c.1920*)

Treforest Jn. looking north towards Pontypridd and the valleys, 9th June, 1952. Horses graze peacefully in the field that was the setting for the hostility between the TVR and CR from 1897 until 1917.

The photograph shows the BR/TVR exchange sidings, the TVR four-road main line, the strip of land purchased by the TVR to obstruct the CR's ambitions, and (centre right) the remains of the CR embankment

Firstly the 1906 Act laid down that the exchange sidings were to be opened simultaneously with the junction and these were never put in, and secondly no record has been traced in the Cardiff or Taff archives of any further traffic. The three parties decided to place the fusion Bills before Parliament again in the 1910 Session, but, due to the continued opposition from Barry and Newport interests, which the Taff was unable to resolve privately, the Bills were withdrawn. Thus in 1910 the Taff and the Cardiff were again facing each other with the junction issue unresolved, but for the time being the matter was left in abeyance because of the Cardiff's financial position.

To obtain some revenue from the new railway it was decided to open it for passenger and local goods traffic. It had been a most difficult and costly railway to construct, as the bed of the Taff valley already accommodated the TVR, the River Taff, the Glamorganshire Canal and the main Merthyr road. Housing and factories occupied much of the remaining area, leaving the Cardiff to wind its way on the extreme eastern side as best it could. According to the Inspecting Officer of the Board of Trade, Lt Col E. Druitt, who inspected the line on 18th October, 1910, the length from Heath Jn on the RR, to the then termination in the field approaching the TVR south of Treforest, was 9 m. 10 ch. This included Rhydyfelin Viaduct (8 m. 71 ch. to 8 m. 79 ch.), 27 overbridges, 15 underbridges and one tunnel, 15 cuttings, several retaining walls and five occupation level crossings.

The viaduct was 512 ft long overall, with rail level 55 ft 10 in. over the river bed. It consisted of four steel girder spans with latticed sides, two of 117 ft 7 in. in length and two at 110 ft 11 in. long. There were masonry abutments at each end, with intermediate piers made from cast iron cylinders filled with concrete and sunk to a depth of 35 ft below the river bed. Five of the bridges were over the main road, and three over the canal, these eight bridges, also the viaduct, having to be built on the skew. Tongwynlais tunnel was 108½ yards long (4 m. 21 ch. to 4 m. 26 ch.) and is said to have been put in at the Marquis's request to shield his vineyard, which stood on the slope at the east side of the railway, in the grounds of Castell Coch, the Marquis's medieval style castle. The thin layer of earth covering the tunnel could easily have been removed to produce yet another cutting. In addition to the earthworks mentioned, the River Taff had to be diverted near Nantgarw, and a feeder constructed for the Treforest Tin Plate works, this having a 33 ft span and a length of 473 ft.

At the time of the inspection the stations for which a contract had been placed on 23rd June, 1910, were not completed, although Col Druitt was well satisfied with the platforms, but instructed that the lighting must be completed before a passenger service commenced.

Coryton, seen on 17th April, 1986; the view is towards the end of the branch.
Bob Pugh

Former CR 0–6–2T No. 155 in the cutting north of Coryton Halt, 16th
August, 1948. *Ian Wright*

Tongwynlais station building and derelict track, looking south on 5th August, 1948. *Ian Wright*

Former RR 0–6–2T No. 66 brushes the weeds aside whilst passing through Tongwynlais with a materials train from Nantgarw on 16th September, 1949. Note the restored medieval Castell Coch on the hillside. *Ian Wright*

The close proximity of the railway, disused Glamorganshire Canal and the River Taff immediately north of Tongwynlais Station, are evident in this photograph, dated 12th April, 1951.   *Ian Wright*

The southern end of Tongwynlais tunnel *c.*1963, ten years after the track had been lifted.   *John White*

However, construction of the proposed halts had not even been started, neither had the two steam rail cars and their trailer cars at this time been delivered, hence the service planned for 14th November was postponed for the time being. Other interesting facts revealed by the report were that the railway was laid double track throughout, with bull head steel rails weighing 86 lb. per yard in 30 ft lengths. The steepest gradient, on the southern approach to Rhydyfelin viaduct, was 1 in 75 and the sharpest curve was of ten chains radius. The deepest cutting had a depth of 68 ft, and the highest embankment was 43 ft 6 in.

Lt Col Druitt made a second inspection on 30th January, 1911, and passed the stations and halts fit for passenger traffic, subject to the stipulation that the halts should be used by single rail cars only. The stations and halts, with mileages from Heath Jn, were – Heath Halt (0 m. 27 ch.) Rhubina Halt (1 m. 74 ch.) Whitchurch Station (2 m. 25 ch.) Coryton Halt (2 m. 58 ch.) Tongwynlais Station (3 m. 63 ch.) Glan-y-Llyn Station (5 m. 44 ch.) Nantgarw Halt (6 m. 31 ch.) Upper Boat Station (7 m. 61 ch.) and Rhyd-y-felin Halt (8 m. 55 ch.). The stations all had both up and down platforms each 450 ft long, with station buildings on the up side, and goods sheds at Whitchurch and Glan-y-Llyn. It had also been intended to put in a goods shed at Upper Boat, but this appears to have been cancelled as an economy measure, although goods sidings were put in there and Tongwynlais. Of the halts the only one with raised platforms was at Heath, where short 50 ft long staggered platforms had been pro- vided. The other lineside halts generally consisted of some ground level timbers, a waiting shed, nameboard, lighting, and a railed fence to keep passengers off the track.

The name originally chosen for Coryton Halt was Asylum but, fortunately, that name was dropped and the new name adopted a short while before the opening date.

A further halt, Portobello (4 m. 60 ch.) had been intended, close to a quarry of that name to be mentioned later, but at the last minute it was decided not to proceed with that halt, the potential traffic pre- sumably not justifying its existence. Two other halts were anticipated once the service had started, these being at Birchgrove (between Heath and Rhubina) and at Treforest, on the approach to the junction with the TVR. Neither of these halts were ever put in by the Cardiff Railway although Birchgrove was added by the GWR in 1929. Doubt- less, construction of a halt at Treforest was continually in abeyance pending the outcome of the exchange sidings issue with the TVR, as it would have had to be sited in the midst of such sidings. Rhubina Halt, which had an occupation level crossing at the southern end, had short raised platforms added in later CR days; also the name was altered to Rhiwbina in 1916, but Coryton, Nantgarw and Rhyd-y-felin remained lineside halts for the remainder of the company's independent existence.

The first steam rail car was delivered by the Gloucester C&W Co. on 23rd February, 1911, and its trailer car a few days later. On 27th February the steam car, with the Marquis and other CR and Gloucester C&W officials on board, made its first trial trip to Rhyd-y-felin and back. As all went well the public service started on 1st March, the southern terminus being the Rhymney Railway station at Cardiff, 1 m. 71 ch. south of Heath Jn.

Initially there was a service of eleven cars each way on weekdays and five each way on Sundays. The second steam car and its trailer were delivered late in March, and this easily sufficed for the traffic. Teething troubles with the cars caused some problems, hence, whenever a car was out of action for repair or servicing, a vacuum fitted loco (usually one of the ex-GWR 0–6–0STs purchased second hand in 1906) worked the service with one trailer car. Meanwhile the CR had applied to join the Railway Clearing House and, with Taff Vale support (!) was accepted on 8th March.

Goods and mineral traffic was also due to start on 1st March, although there was little traffic initially. A siding had been put into a brick works at Birchgrove, and a further siding into Portobello Quarry already mentioned. However, until coal had been wrested from the TVR at Treforest, the company's main traffic hopes lay with a colliery Thomas Taylor – a local contractor and owner of barges on the canal – had started sinking at Nantgawr in 1910. During that year Taylor signed an agreement with the CR for the latter to put in a siding to the east side of the main line to his colliery. A ground frame was provided at 6 m. 42 ch. to control the siding. On 23rd October, 1912 Taylor reached the Three Feet seam of steam coal at a depth of 470 yards, but decided to sink deeper to the richer steam coal seams. These were not reached until 1915, at a depth of 856 yards, making Nantgawr (then better known as Taylor's Pit) the deepest colliery in South Wales at the time. However, due to wartime conditions, with many miners serving in the colours, coupled with wet conditions at the pit, despatch of coal for the first few years was insignificant, amounting only to some 500 to 600 tons per week, which traffic was easily taken away by the daily pick up goods.

With the railway losing money, and the docks producing only a very modest dividend despite its massive steam coal export trade (Parliament having refused to authorise an increase in dock charges in 1913), the shareholders became very angry and demanded that the junction be completed at Treforest to enable them to share in the profits then being made by the TVR from the coal trade, which reached its peak in 1913. Hence in May of that year Col C.S. Denniss, the Cardiff's general manager, obtained permission from his Board to re-open negotiations with the Taff. In view of the company's financial position he suggested a modified junction to save expense but, after the usual drawn out skirmishes the Taff rejected his proposal. On 6th July, 1914 a Notice of Treat was served on the Taff to enable the CR to acquire, by lease, the parcel of land required to effect the junction. The Taff objected to the levels shown on the Cardiff plan, saying that the fifteen feet high embankment which the Cardiff had already put in across the field approaching the Taff line would, if extended across the Taff's strip of land, obstruct any siding which they might put in alongside their main line on the strip.

After further months of argument the CR insisted on their right to such lease, quoting the authorisation given in the 1906 Act, coupled with the mode of junction confirmed by the Arbitration award two years later. On this occasion the Taff resorted to litigation asking the Court to declare that the CR were not entitled to an easement over the strip of land which they had purchased adjacent to their main line. The case was heard before Mr Justice Astbury in the Court of Chancery on 11th July, 1916. It upheld the Cardiff's arguments and dismissed the Taff's action. That was still not the end of the matter as the TVR took the matter to the Court of Appeal where, on 10th November, 1916, battle was renewed. Ten days later the Master of the Rolls gave his judgement which, to everyone's surprise, reversed the judgement of the lower court. He said that, whilst the CR certainly had authority to make a junction, it was not up to them to make it in the most burdensome manner, and deprive the Taff of the use of the land they had purchased. With success still eluding them 19 years after the Act of authorisation had been granted, the Cardiff felt there was no alternative but to appeal to the House of Lords.

However, before such appeal was scheduled to be heard, a somewhat similar situation arose as in 1908/9; behind the scenes the Boards of the TVR, CR and RR met to discuss a closer working relationship, as the principal railway companies concerned with the trade at Cardiff docks. It was agreed that a unified management was essential and, as none of the parties wished a repeat of the Fusion Bills failures of 1909/10, such had to be achieved by agreement and without Parliamentary approval. It was decided that Mr E.A. Prosser, until earlier in 1917 the general manager of the RR, was the man to head the management team, as Mr Beasley – the Taff's GM and the 1909 choice – was shortly due for retirement. Mr Prosser had been seconded to the War Office as Deputy Director of Railway Movements on 15th January, 1917, but was released to resume his duties with the RR as

The 1.05 pm railmotor (No. 3) ex Rhydyfelin, with driving trailer No. 4 leading, between Portobello and Tongwynlais tunnel; 20th May, 1919.

Locomotive Club of Great Britain

During the alterations at 5m. 33ch. an 0–6–2T, with coal from Nantgarw Colliery, passes over the temporary girder bridge on 8th May, 1952.

British Rail

Looking south from 5 m 33 ch. on 8th May 1952. The temporary girder bridge is on the left, and the new spur under construction to Taffs Well on the right.

British Rail

0–6–2T No. 5622 heads a train of empties for Nantgarw Colliery over the new link from Taffs Well, TVR section, May 1957.

Derek Chaplin

from 1st April. The previous day Mr Denniss, the Cardiff's GM, resigned, enabling Mr Prosser to return to manage both companies. It only remained for the Taff to join in. On 4th July a grateful Taff Board elected Mr Beasley to a seat on the Board as Managing Director, and two days later the agreement between the three companies was signed, with Mr Prosser appointed as the Taff's GM from the same date. Thus after some 60 years of almost unceasing conflict between the parties, wartime conditions had brought them together under a common management.

Nevertheless the Treforest junction dispute was still awaiting hearing by the Lords of Appeal. Under the new arrangements neither party wished to prolong the dispute hence, to tie up the loose ends, the Taff nominally accepted the Notice of Treat, which allowed the Cardiff to withdraw their appeal and recover the deposited costs. Both parties fully understood that was the end of the matter, and nothing would be done regarding putting in the junction. Thus ended the Cardiff's dream of becoming the largest combined dock and railway undertaking in South Wales, and left the company with a comparatively short length of main line which, as one paper reported, "started nowhere and finished nowhere, in a field actually".

The policy of unified management worked well in the difficult conditions towards the latter end of the War, and on 9th January, 1919 a meeting was held between representatives of the three companies, with representatives of the Barry Railway. At that meeting it was decided that a joint committee be set up consisting of not more than two Directors from each company, to view the principle of complete amalgamation between the four companies, on the basis of either the gross or nett revenue of each company for the eight years ending 31st December, 1914. Nothing has been traced about any further meetings, it seems probable that these were discontinued once it became known that the Government intended to introduce its own railways amalgamation Bill.

Returning to the Cardiff Railway passenger service, this was severely cut back for a while in 1912 as an economy measure, but increased again over the years to something approaching the opening service. By 1920 there were ten trains each way on weekdays, half of which were available for workmen's tickets and four each way on Sundays.

With the return to peacetime conditions the Taylor's Navigation Steam Coal Co. was formed to develop Nantgarw Colliery, and on 31st March, 1920 the new company took over Thomas Taylor's agreement with the CR. Early in 1921 the company advised the railway company that they would require additional sidings at Nantgarw to deal with the anticipated traffic, and by April of that year the CR had produced a plan of the proposed new layout. This was accepted by the colliery company, and the sidings laid during the latter half of the summer, leading to a revised agreement signed between the parties on 12th September, 1921.

The existing siding to the colliery became Nantgawr South Jn, and a new North Jn at 6 m. 69 ch. was added, with extensive sidings (on the down side of the CR) between the two junctions for loaded and empty wagons. An elevated signal box was put in on the up side of the main line, sited mid-way between the junctions, this replaced the ground frame that previously controlled the old junction. Despite the extensive work carried out coal output did not increase dramatically, an average of some 2000 tons per week being despatched in 1922, rising to an average of nearly 2500 tons per week the following year. One train per day was sufficient to cope with such traffic in the final year of the CR's independent existence, although a path for a second train was included in the timetable, if such was needed.

Resulting from the Railways Act of 19th August, 1921 the CR was, on account of its extensive dock undertaking, included as an amalgamated company in the GWR group, and came under Paddington control as from 25th March, 1922. Thus it was left to the GWR to decide the fate of the unfinished junction at Treforest. At that time the export coal trade was gradually recovering from the restrictions due to the War, but still far below the pre-War boom, hence no hasty decision was taken pending the return of more settled conditions. By 1925 it had become obvious that the demand for steam coal was declining. Hence, as the existing Taff lines could easily cope with the traffic, on 16th September, 1925 the former CR north of Rhydyfelin (from 8 m. 70 ch.) was taken out of use and lifted the following year. The CR had laid their rails to 9 m. 26 ch., but the GW closure also nominally included to the unfinished junction (9 m. 28 ch.) despite the temporary junction having been removed late in 1909. For some years, probably since 1917, the CR had ceased maintenance north of 9 m. 0 ch., but despite this an early post-grouping GW record listed Treforest Halt at 9 m. 21 ch., marked "no platforms, never used". Whether such halt physically existed is problematical, despite the wording suggesting that it did.

Another feature following the Railways Act was that the Marquis of Bute's private sidings in the East Moors area of the docks (see Docks section), were purchased by the GWR as from 1st January, 1922 by agreement dated 22nd February, 1923. As these sidings were always worked by the CR, such purchase was the only logical course. As many of the stations and halts taken over by the GWR (particularly in

Wagons stored on the disused CR section between Tongwynlais and south of the 5m. 33ch. alterations, seen on 24th August, 1952. Note the former Barry Railway Walnut Tree viaduct in the background.   *Eric Parker*

Slewing old track and laying new track for the double line Nantgarw Colliery branch at Glanyllyn, April 1952.   *Ian Wright*

0–6–2T No. 6672 eases a train of Nantgarw coal through the long closed Glanyllyn Station towards the new link on 20th April, 1965.   *John White*

The disused Cardiff Railway looking south, showing Nantgarw Colliery North Jn, 23rd April, 1937. Note the light narrow gauge track laid between the old main lines, on which a small petrol engine ferried materials for the preparation of the site for the Treforest Trading Estate. *Steve Rowson Collection*

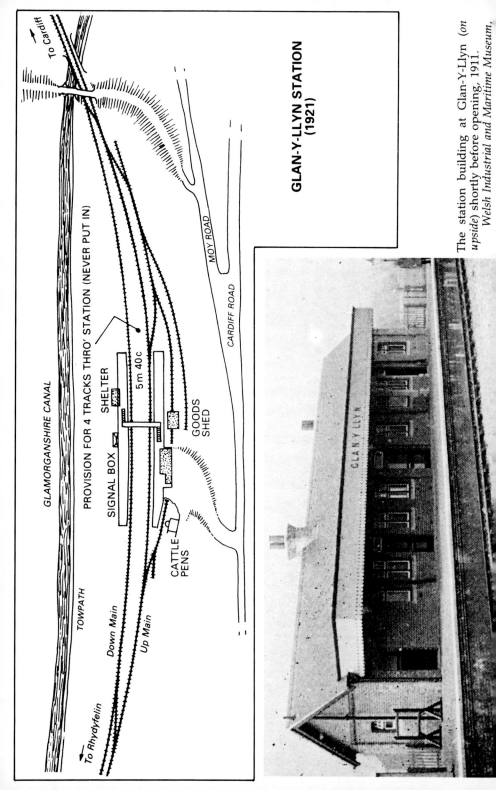

GLAN-Y-LLYN STATION
(1921)

To Cardiff

GLAMORGANSHIRE CANAL

TOWPATH

Down Main

Up Main

To Rhydyfelin

PROVISION FOR 4 TRACKS THRO' STATION (NEVER PUT IN)

SHELTER

SIGNAL BOX

5m 40c

CATTLE
PENS

GOODS
SHED

MOY ROAD

CARDIFF ROAD

The station building at Glan-Y-Llyn (*on upside*) shortly before opening, 1911. *Welsh Industrial and Maritime Museum,*

GLAN·Y·LLYN

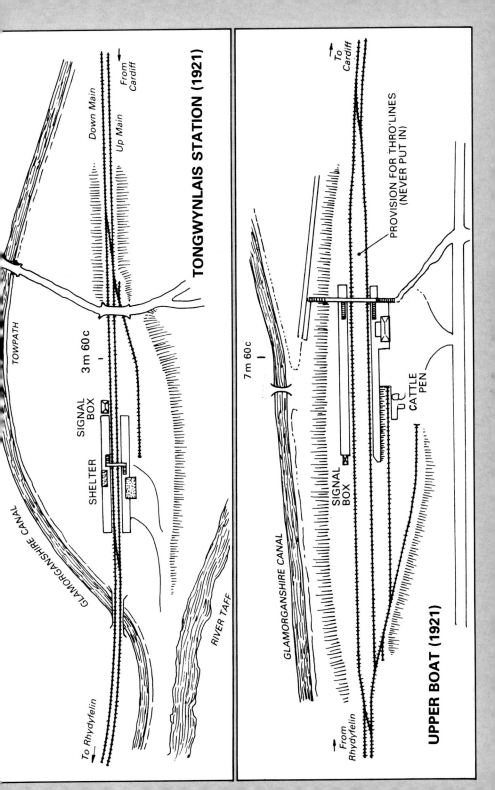

TONGWYNLAIS STATION (1921)

From Cardiff

Down Main

Up Main

TOWPATH

GLAMORGANSHIRE CANAL

3 m 60 c

SIGNAL BOX

SHELTER

RIVER TAFF

To Rhydyfelin

UPPER BOAT (1921)

To Cardiff

PROVISION FOR THRO' LINES
(NEVER PUT IN)

7 m 60 c

GLAMORGANSHIRE CANAL

SIGNAL BOX

CATTLE PEN

From Rhydyfelin

Tongwynlais Station as seen on 16th, December 1967. *John White*

Derelict Upper Boat Station as seen on 22nd, September 1963. *John White*

South Wales) bore similar names to nearby or existing GWR stations, these were clarified by partial renaming on 1st July, 1924. Those on the former CR affected were – with the revised names – Heath Halt (Low Level), Whitchurch (Glam) Station, Coryton (Glam) Halt and Rhydyfelin Halt (Low Level).

Nantgarw Colliery reached its peak output during 1923/4. Some 860 people were employed there, and two trains were run each night to clear the traffic. The following year the Taff Rhondda Navigation Steam Coal Co. purchased the colliery, but the modest boom was not destined to last. Serious geological problems coupled with the effects of the prolonged miners' strike in 1926 dealt it a mortal blow, and it was closed entirely the following year. With the principal traffic on the line gone, and passenger traffic beyond the outskirts of Cardiff reduced to negligible proportions, the GWR had to make economies. On 16th May, 1928 they singled the line from just north of Whitchurch Station (from 2 m. 37 ch.) to the terminus north of Rhydyfelin Halt (8 m. 70 ch.). The old up line was retained with passing loops at Tongwynlais, Nantgarw Colliery, Upper Boat and Rhydyfelin. A platform was erected on the up side at the latter place (at 8 m. 63 ch.), also a platform on the down side at Nantgarw (6 m. 28 ch.) these replacing the lineside halts. The down platforms at Tongwynlais, Glanyllyn and Upper Boat were taken out of use, but at the southern end of the line the platforms at Heath Halt had been extended in 1923.

However, these economies did not achieve the desired result. For the year 1930, at the height of the depression, the total combined receipts from the stations and halts north of Coryton, for passenger, goods and minerals, only amounted to £1521 – less than £30 per week. Hence it was not surprising that this section of the branch, from 2 m. 65 ch. was closed as from 20th July, 1931. In March 1928 the Powell Duffryn Steam Coal Co. – the largest in South Wales – had purchased Nantgarw Colliery from the liquidators of the Taff Rhondda Co., and had signed an agreement with the GWR to confirm their position in relation to that colliery. This agreement was terminated by the railway company on 17th October, 1931, as was the Portobello Quarry agreement from which there had also been no traffic since 1927, but they agreed to leave the line *in situ* pending a decision by Powell Duffryn as to the future of the colliery, realising nothing was likely to result until the depression had lifted.

At the southern end of the line commuter traffic from Whitchurch and the halts to Cardiff kept at a reasonably high level during the slump, and a new two platform halt was opened at Birchgrove (1 m. 35 ch.) on 10th June, 1929. The platforms at Heath Halt were again extended about 1930 to take five coach trains, and Rhiwbina Halt had its platforms extended at much the same time. Only Coryton was left as a ground level halt until the 1931 closure. That halt was of course on the short remaining section of single line north of Whitchurch, and when it became the terminus of the passenger service, a platform was put in on the up side, immediately south of the road overbridge (2 m. 56 ch.), although the mileage remained unaltered in the WTTs for several years. As auto trains were working the service this section of single line caused no problems, but shortly afterwards seaside and football excursions were run from the branch, and these had to start and terminate at Whitchurch until a run around loop was put in at Coryton on 23rd July, 1932, permitting ordinary trains to use the halt.

No further changes took place in the 1930s, the commuter service increased its traffic, and a daily goods train cleared the traffic at Whitchurch and a brickworks and a couple of factories in the Birchgrove area. North of Coryton the track remained *in situ*, probably not in use, although this cannot be taken as certain as the GWR included, in their working appendix, a paragraph detailing the regulations for trains working north of Coryton. It is possible the line was used for wagon storage during that period, but confirmation is lacking. Early in 1938 the Powell Duffryn Associated Collieries Ltd (as reconstituted 8.1936) intimated that they intended to develop Nantgarw Colliery, and letters were exchanged between the company and the GWR on 14th February, 1938 re-opening the agreement that had been cancelled late in 1931. By the summer of 1939 an occasional train of materials ran up the line to the colliery, and spasmodic workings are known to have continued until 1944 at least. Some of these trains carried slurry from other Powell Duffryn collieries to the Nantgarw site. The single line section north of Nantgarw was used for wagon storage prior to its removal (7 m. 20 ch. to 8 m. 70 ch.) on 26th October, 1940. Rhydyfelin Viaduct was taken down in 1943 and yielded 1500 tons of steel for the War effort.

In common with most other branch lines, the Coryton passenger service was severely curtailed at the outbreak of War, but was fairly quickly restored to almost pre-War level. War time conditions saw ambulance trains on the branch. A couple of hospitals were within easy reach of Whitchurch station and the latter, with its extensive platforms, was suitable to deal with the situation.

Peacetime conditions saw the Powell Duffryn Co. preparing plans for major development at Nantgarw and these plans, for a modern colliery complex with coke ovens and a by-product plant, were approved by the Ministry of Fuel and Power in 1946. Following nationalisation of the mines as from 1st January, 1947 the NCB carried on with PDs plans and by late 1947 trains of materials and equipment again passed up the old Cardiff line, initially about one train per week. The only signal box available to cover such workings north of Coryton was at Whitchurch and, with the passenger service extending north of the box to Coryton Halt, the mode of train working was far from simple. A staff existed for the single line section, Whitchurch to Coryton, but this could not be retained by freight trains working to Nantgarw and back, as it was needed for the passenger service. To get over the problem a traffic man accompanied each goods train from Whitchurch box to catch points protecting Coryton Halt from the north. Beyond the catch points three detonators were strapped to the track and the train proceeded to Nantgarw. The man returned to Whitchurch box with the staff, and then returned to Coryton to await the train's return. On arrival it was stopped short of the detonators and had to wait there until the man had walked to Whitchurch box again, collected the staff, and returned to the waiting train. He also collected the key for the Coryton ground frame, and thus was able to set the catch points to allow the train to proceed over the run around loop at Coryton and on to Whitchurch where the staff and ground frame key were returned.

With such few trains running to Nantgarw this cumbersome but necessary method of working presented no serious problem, but once coal started flowing down line in 1951 an improved method had to be devised. Hence a temporary mode of working was introduced on Tuesday 28th August, 1951. Trains to/from Nantgarw were confined to the period between 9.30 am and 4.30 pm and during those hours Coryton Halt was closed to traffic, and the passenger service terminated at Whitchurch. This allowed the single line section from Whitchurch to Nantgarw to be cleared as one section, and the staff to be carried to the colliery and back.

This was regarded purely as a temporary measure, as work had already commenced linking the northern end of the former Cardiff Railway with the former TVR just north of Taffs Well Station. This link was very similar, although in the reverse direction, to that proposed by the TVR in their 1902 and 1903 Bills. On those occasions the proposed link was in the down direction from the Taff, whilst the link under construction started at 5 m. 33 ch. on the Cardiff section (south of Glan-y-Llyn Station) and fed down to the Taff Vale section at Nantgarw Colliery Branch Jn (7 m. 30 ch. Taff section mileage).

In order to keep coal flowing whilst the work was being carried out at 5 m. 33 ch., a temporary loop was put in around that point. This necessitated a temporary girder bridge having to be erected over the

The same site as the lower photograph on page 75, as seen on 3rd March, 1952, showing the new Nantgarw Colliery and Coke Ovens, and new North Jn. *British Rail*

The dereliction at the Upper Boat Station site is evident on 30th July, 1960. The wide separation of up and down platforms illustrates the 1910 dream of coal trains and empties using the centre roads, whilst a passenger train could stand at a platform. *M. Hale*

Rhydyfelin terminus in June 1921, with signal cabin, somersault signals, water tank and run around loop, but lacking a platform. *Courtesy Brian Miller*

Testing Rhydyfelin viaduct with Cardiff Railway and Rhymney Railway locomotives on both roads, October 1910.

Welsh Industrial and Maritime Museum, Cardiff

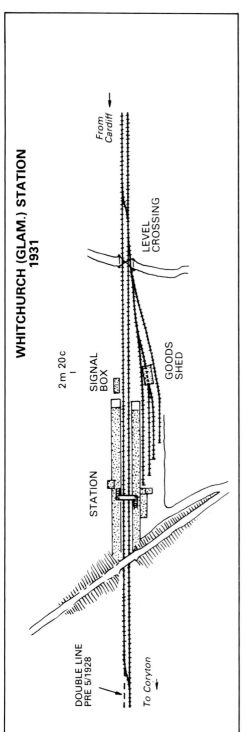

WHITCHURCH (GLAM.) STATION
1931

2 m 20c

STATION

SIGNAL
BOX

GOODS
SHED

LEVEL
CROSSING

From Cardiff

To Coryton

DOUBLE LINE
PRE 5/1928

Right: The main Whitchurch
Station building (*on upside*) from
the outside, March 1956.
Derek Chaplin

The Goods Shed at Whitchurch Station seen here in March 1956.
Derek Chaplin

Selection of buttons and lapel badge.   *Derek Robinson and Ken Good*

old canal, by that time in complete disuse. The original Cardiff line was slewed over a couple of yards westwards to suit the link line alignment from Taffs Well. When completed and opened for traffic on 16th June, 1952 the link and the former CR section from 5 m. 33 ch. to 7 m. 18 ch. was double track, the two chains to 7 m. 20 ch. being taken out from the same date in connection with the revised siding layout at Nantgarw. A new ground level signal box to control the colliery sidings was also installed.

The single line north of Coryton (from 2 m. 65 ch. to 5 m. 33 ch.) was taken out of use for traffic purposes at the same time, but for a year or so continued to be used for wagon storage, and was finally lifted in October 1953. After 16th June, 1952 there was no actual connection between the single line and the new Nantgarw Colliery branch, as the temporary bridge and loop were removed directly the new link was opened.

In the early 1960s considerable doubt existed as to the future of the Coryton branch. In 1962 the passenger service was severely cut, whilst private sidings agreements in the Birchgrove area were terminated on 30th June, 1963. Whitchurch goods shed closed as from 2nd October, 1963, the traffic that remained being dealt with at the main depot at Cardiff. In the latter half of 1963 the branch, along with several other branches in South Wales was put up for complete closure, but strong opposition from the select residential area of north Cardiff saved the day and the closure, planned for 15th June, 1964, was not approved. However, Whitchurch Station was unstaffed from that date, and virtually became just another halt on the branch.

With diesel multiple units working the passenger service the run around loop at Coryton was taken out of use on 15th October, 1964, followed by the shortening of the branch to the end of Coryton platform (2 m. 56 ch.) on 27th October, 1964. Under the Cardiff MAS scheme the entire branch, apart from the double line junction at Heath, was singled as from 25th July, 1966. The former up line was taken out of use, leaving all platforms on the down side except at Coryton, where the single platform was on the up side. As from 5th May, 1969 the suffix "Halt" was dropped, leaving those on the Coryton branch (as elsewhere) re-classified as stations.

The Nantgarw Colliery branch was singled as from 25th November, 1973, the existing section of the former Cardiff Railway north of 5 m. 33 ch. being unusual in that it was opened as double track, singled in 1928, re-doubled in 1952, and again singled in 1973. Although some doubts have been expressed as to the future of the colliery, in any case the coke ovens should secure the future of the branch for the foreseeable future.

There were plans in the late 1970s to replace the double line junction at Heath with a single line junction and crossover. One such scheme involved the closure of both Heath HL and LL stations with a new station, serving both Cardiff and Rhymney sections, being put in on the other (or south) side of the road serving the present stations. These schemes came to nought, but on 19th November, 1984 a new Heath Jn was effected. Between the former Heath Jn and the road bridges in Heath Halt Road, the former CR and RR sections ran parallel for just over a quarter of a mile, the RR line climbing at 1 in 80 towards its Heath HL Station.

A property development company entered into negotiations with BR to take over the former CR land between the points mentioned, this included an area near the junction on which a number of sidings formerly stood. It has been stated that some 45 dwellings will be built on the site. To enable a link to be put in near the road bridges, the different levels on the two sections necessitated a gradient of 1 in 50 falling towards the CR section. The new Heath Jn is at 3 m. 32 ch. on the Rhymney section, fourteen chains further north than the old junction. From there the new link, nine chains long, drops sharply to join the former CR section at 0 m. 25 ch. almost under the road bridge mentioned, only three chains south of Heath LL Station. In effect this shortens the Coryton branch by 16 chains, although the actual length of former Cardiff Railway mileage is reduced by 25 chains, to 2 m. 31 ch. A single line junction with the up Rhymney line was put in, with crossover to the down Rhymney. The old Heath Jn signal box (3 m. 23 ch.) was taken out of use the same day, and replaced by a small lineside cabin opposite the new junction. The old semaphore signals were replaced by colour lights (both sections) and the branch is now controlled electronically, replacing the former single line staff control.

On the closed section between Coryton and 5 m. 33 ch. the new Cardiff to Merthyr trunk road swept away much of the old CR formation in the Taffs Well area, including Tongwynlais Tunnel, in 1970. Upper Boat station building, which was in a derelict condition for several years, disappeared about ten years later, whilst Glan-y-Llyn station building, alongside the Nantgarw Colliery branch, still exists as a private residence. At the northern end the embankment in the field approaching the TVR section, where the Cardiff Railway ended up, still stands as a monument to a failed enterprise.

Thus all that now (1985) remains of the railway on which the Marquis and his friends pinned such high hopes is two short single line sections, the north Cardiff commuter service on the Coryton branch (0 m. 25 ch. to 2 m. 56 ch.) and coal traffic on the northern section of the Nantgarw Colliery branch (5 m. 33 ch. to 7 m. 18 ch.).

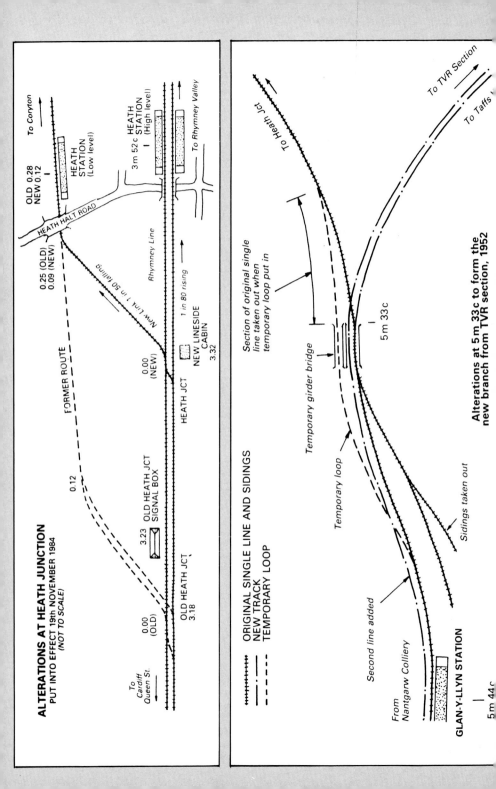

ALTERATIONS AT HEATH JUNCTION
PUT INTO EFFECT 19th NOVEMBER 1984
(NOT TO SCALE)

To Coryton

HEATH STATION (Low level)

OLD 0.28
NEW 0.12

HEATH HALT ROAD

0.25 (OLD)
0.09 (NEW)

FORMER ROUTE

0.12

0.00 (OLD)

To Cardiff Queen St.

3.23 OLD HEATH JCT SIGNAL BOX

OLD HEATH JCT 3.18

New Link 1 in 50 falling

Rhymney Line

0.00 (NEW)

HEATH JCT

1 in 80 rising

NEW LINESIDE CABIN 3.32

3 m 52 c HEATH STATION (High level)

To Rhymney Valley

┿┿┿┿┿┿ ORIGINAL SINGLE LINE AND SIDINGS
─·─·─·─ NEW TRACK
─ ─ ─ ─ TEMPORARY LOOP

Alterations at 5 m 33c to form the new branch from TVR section, 1952

To TVR Section

To Taffs

To Heath Jct

Section of original single line taken out when temporary loop put in

Temporary girder bridge

Temporary loop

5 m 33c

Sidings taken out

Second line added

From Nantgarw Colliery

GLAN-Y-LLYN STATION

5 m 44c

There is a further scheme, now well advanced which, if approved in its entirety, will revitalise the Coryton branch service by introducing a through service between Coryton and Radyr, with the city centre as its pivot.

At present referred to as the Inner City Service, trains from the Coryton branch would proceed to Cardiff Queen St as at present, thence around the loop to Cardiff Central, on to Ninian Park, proceeding to Radyr via the former Taff Vale line (Penarth Dock and Harbour section).

New stations would be provided at:

A. TY GLAS – between Heath LL and Birchgrove on the Coryton Branch. (The station is due to open in January 1987 in advance of the main scheme.)
B. NINIAN PARK – where the present "football platforms" would be rebuilt into a modern station.
C. WAUNGRON ROAD, FAIRWATER and DANESCOURT, sited on the PD&H section between Ninian Park and Radyr.

This semi-circular city service, some 9½ miles in length and covering 13 stations, would cater for the densely populated areas to the north, west and north west of the city, passing through the city centre and its two principal railway stations en route, and should prove a great convenience to the public.

It is hoped the service will start by Autumn 1987, with a half hourly service planned during the day.

However, to conclude the railway section, a brief summary of closures and singling may be helpful.

m. ch.		m. ch.		
0	0	to 0	25	Taken out of use, and lifted, on the opening of the new Heath Jn 19th November, 1984.
0	25	to 2	56	Still in use, Coryton branch.
2	56	to 2	65	Taken out of use, and lifted 27th October, 1964.
2	65	to 5	33	Closed to traffic 16th June, 1952. Used for wagon storage until lifted October 1953.
5	33	to 7	18	Still in use as part of the Nantgarw Colliery branch.
7	18	to 7	20	Taken out of use and lifted 16th June, 1952.
7	20	to 8	70	Closed 20th July, 1931. Used for wagon storage until lifted 26th October, 1940.
8	70	to 9	26	(North of Rhydyfelin Halt) Closed 16th September, 1925. Lifted 1926.
9	26	to 9	28	(Treforest (Cardiff Jn) with TVR) Closed and lifted by authority of the TVR Board 12th October, 1909. Nominally closed by the GWR 16th September, 1925.
0	12	to 2	37	Singled as from 25th July, 1966.
2	37	to 8	70	Singled as from 6th May, 1928.
5	33	to 7	18	Re-doubled, as part of Nantgarw Colliery branch, 16th June, 1952.
5	33	to 7	18	Singled again as from 25th November, 1973.

Rhydyfelin viaduct, over which only one train ever ran (a ceremonial coal train on 15th May, 1909); as standing on 14th October, 1935. *British Rail*

STOP PRESS ON PUBLICATION

On Monday 13th October (1986) British Coal announced its intention to close Nantgarw Colliery, subject to the normal closure procedure, the reason given being the uncertain geology at Nantgarw. The closure involves some 650 miners being made redundant.

In view of the generous redundancy terms now being offered, which are due to be drastically reduced in the next few months, the NUM are not opposing the closure, hence it seems probable that Nantgarw will finally close late in December 1986.

Initially the associated Coke Ovens at Nantgarw were not affected, but a fortnight later (27th October) National Smokeless Fuels – a subsidiary of British Coal – announced that closure also, scheduled for early in 1987. This will make a further 190 men redundant.

Hence it would appear that the Nantgarw Colliery branch will also close later in 1987 and, as this includes the last part of the northern section of the former Cardiff Railway (*see page 89*), it will leave only the Coryton branch still in use.

Part Three

Locomotives, Rolling Stock and Operations

LOCOMOTIVES

It is only possible to piece together an outline history of the early Bute locos as, being privately owned, few records of such now exist, as is the case with most railway companies. What is known has been detailed in the RCTS "Locomotives of the GWR" Part 10, hence it is only necessary to give an outline summary within the confines of this book. It has never been established with any degree of certainty when the Bute Trustees first employed their (own) locomotives on the docks, but this would appear to have been very late 1860 or early 1861, when the first known engines Nos. 3 and 4 arrived.

Until the Summer of 1859 all the lines within the dock area had been put in by the railway companies themselves, who worked the traffic thereon, including those to the coaling tips, or staithes as they were generally referred to in those days. The Trustees completed their own high level loop line around the north end of the new East Dock in July 1859 (known as the Viaduct branch) to enable coal traffic being handled by the Rhymney Railway (most of it from Taff Vale territory) to be tipped at the staithes on the west side, without the TVR handling it again. It would appear that, although the RR worked the coal traffic around the viaduct branch, other transfer traffic was handled by the Trustees themselves. Hence locomotives No. 1 and 2 were the ones that probably worked that traffic, possibly hired from the contractors who built the branch. This seems the only reasonable explanation, as the first two locomotives known to have been purchased by the Trustees were numbered 3 and 4.

These two engines were 0-6-0STs, Beyer Peacock & Co. Nos. 201 and 202, with 14 in. inside cylinders, 4 ft wheels, and worked at a pressure of 120 psi. No. 3 is said to have been delivered in December 1860, and No. 4 in January 1861. A third engine, No. 5 was an 0-4-0ST with outside cylinders. This was Manning Wardle No. 46, and with 2 ft 9 in. wheels and short wheelbase would have been a very useful machine to work with light loads around the sharp curves at wharves and so on. No. 5 was delivered in February 1862.

Meanwhile a dock mechanical engineering workshop had been built at Tyndall Street, at the NW corner of the East Dock, in 1861. This included space for locomotive repairs, and one small section was used as an engine shed. It was not until 1881 that a purpose built loco. shed was erected at East Moors, sited on the eastern side of the East Dock, and but a short distance from the Rhymney Railways' main engine shed.

No. 6 loco appears to have been Manning Wardle No. 82, an

0–6–0ST with 12 in. inside cylinders and 3 ft 1½ in. wheels which was delivered new to a Cardiff firm in 1863, but acquired by the Trustees a year or two later.

By their 1866 Act, which authorised construction of the Roath Basin, the Trustees acquired powers not only to build their own line to the new basin, and work the traffic there themselves, but also to work the traffic *free of charge* at the tip and wharf roads of the earlier docks; the railway companies to place and collect traffic at nearby sidings. This did not apply to the east side of the West Dock as that was, as stated earlier, leased to the Taff Vale Railway. This somewhat foolish and costly piece of legislation was repealed in 1882. One further locomotive, No. 7, was purchased new in August 1866 to help in this work. This was a further Manning Wardle inside cylinder 0–6–0T, their No. 173, which looked somewhat antiquated with its fluted dome cover and Salter spring balance safety valves. However, this larger engine, with 15 in. cylinders and 4 ft wheels, had performed exactly 50 years of hard work at the docks when it was finally sold, in September 1916, to a dealer for further use by the Government.

The last of the early assortment of locomotives, No. 8, arrived in March 1868. Once again the Trustees purchased an inside cylinder 0–6–0T from Manning Wardle (No. 230) but this was a much smaller engine, the cylinders only of 13 in. diameter and the wheels 3 ft. It was not as useful as No. 7 and was replaced in 1899.

Possibly as a result of No. 8 not proving a good investment, the Trustees embarked upon a modest programme of standardisation for the next few years, which resulted in thirteen further inside cylinder 0–6–0STs being supplied to them by a local engineering firm, Parfitt and Jenkins, whose premises were but a stone's throw from the Tyndall Street Depot. These small but quite powerful locos had 15½ in. cylinders, 4 ft wheels, worked at 160 psi and their full length tanks held 1000 gallons of water. Although some of the building dates are not known exactly (as indicated) all were constructed between 1869 and 1881 as follows: No. 9 (1869), Nos. 10 and 11 (1870/1), 12 (1871), 14 (1872), 15 and 16 (1873), 18 and 19 (1875), 20 and 21 (1877–9), 22 (1880), and 23 (1881). These became the standard dock shunters for many years, and four survived to pass into GW hands in 1922, these were Nos. 12 (GW 694), 15 (695), 18 (696) and 19 (697). Of these No. 15 had a complete rebuild as late as April 1922 when it had a new boiler and tubes, new cylinders and new tyres. It survived as such until a mass withdrawal of absorbed locomotive stock took place on 30th October, 1926, at the start of the slump which followed the General and Miners' strike of that year. It was placed on the Sales List but, finding no buyers, was cut up at Swindon in October 1928.

0–6–0ST No. 12, constructed by Parfitt & Jenkins 1872 for the Bute Trustees. The oldest CR engine still at work (in original condition) at the 1922 amalgamation; became GW 694. *Real Photographs*

0–6–0ST No. 22 (P&J 1880) shunting at the docks *c.*1906; withdrawn 1908.
F. Equeall

0–6–0ST GW No. 697 (CR No. 19) built by P&J in 1875. Photographed at the docks on 14th August, 1924. *Lens of Sutton*

0–6–0PT No. 2, built by Kitson 1882; became GW No. 693, withdrawn January 1925. *Real Photographs*

0–6–0ST No. 24, of uncertain origin. Allotted GW No. 698 but withdrawn in
May 1922. Here she is seen at the docks in January 1920.

The late W. Beckerlegge

The first locomotive delivered to the Bute Docks Co. was 0–6–2T No. 27
(Kitson 1887) seen here shunting at the docks as GW No. 162, *c*.1926.

Real Photographs

It will be noticed that two numbers in the locomotive list, 13 and 17, have not been dealt with. Nothing at all is known about No. 13, but whatever engine carried that number could only have been at Cardiff Docks from 1871/2 until another No. 13 arrived in 1882. Loco No. 17 was a further small 0-4-0ST with 11 in. outside cylinders and 2 ft 10 in. wheels. It was supplied by Fox, Walker and Co. of Bristol (Works No. 200) in June 1874 and, as was the case with the other 0-4-0STs, did a lot of useful work in an area full of sharp curves before being sold for further use to the Government in September 1916.

About 1882 there was a change of policy by the Trustees, five of the following six engines were purchased second hand, and newly acquired engines were given vacant running numbers from earlier engines withdrawn from service, or renumbered. Initially No. 3 was renumbered No. 1 to fill one of the gaps that had existed since the very early Bute engines. The other vacant number (2) was filled by a new arrival from Messrs Kitson of Leeds (No. 2458) in 1882. This odd looking engine was an 0-6-0 pannier tank of the long boilered type with 17 in. inside cylinders and 4 ft 2½ in. diameter wheels. It had a short wheelbase, with long overhang at the rear end. Somehow it lasted to become GWR No. 693, but was sent by Swindon to the makers for overhaul in December 1924, but its condition resulted in it being cut up at Leeds, and the sections returned to Swindon in wagons, in February 1925.

The next three engines were inside cylinder 4-4-0 side tanks purchased second hand from the North London Railway. They are believed to have been built by Slaughter, Gruning and Co. of Bristol, in 1861 and had 16½ in. diameter cylinders. With coupled wheels 5 ft 3 in. in diameter, it is difficult to envisage what use could be made with them for dock work. They were given Bute Nos. 3, 6 and 13 when received in 1882/3, the old No. 3 having been renumbered 1, and old No. 6 sold to a contractor at Newport. The three 4-4-0Ts did not last long, and they were replaced in 1895, 1899 and 1895 respectively.

In 1883 a further oddity arrived at the docks and was given the number 24. This is reputed to have been a 2-4-2ST when it was transferred from the Bute colliery at Hirwaun to the docks. It is said to have been built as an 0-4-2T by Beyer Peacock and Co. about 1860, although practically nothing is known of its early days. It was rebuilt at Tyndall Street as an 0-6-0T in 1885 and, as such, lasted to pass into GWR hands in 1922. At the time it was laid up for heavy overhaul, hence it was despatched to Swindon in May 1922 and promptly cut up there. In the general renumbering scheme some three months later, it was allotted GW No. 698, but by that time its "bits and pieces" had long since been melted down in the furnaces for new construction.

The Trustees' No. 25 was an even greater oddity. This was an 0–6–0ST with a French origin. Originally built as an 0–6–0 tender engine in the 1850s, it was sold to Brassey, the contractor, in 1858. At some time it was altered to an 0–6–0ST, and worked on the East and West Jn Railway. It was purchased by the Trustees in 1885, and renumbered 32 in 1907. It was one of the six engines sold to dealers for Government use in September 1916.

With the prospect of increased coal traffic when the Roath Dock was completed, the Trustees reverted to purchasing new robust engines. The first of these, No. 26, was received at Cardiff in 1886. It was an 0–6–2 side tank of more modern design, with overall cab and a proper bunker which held 45 cwt of coal. Until that time practically all the loco stock had arrived without cab roofs and either with a very small bunker, or none at all, the coal having to be stored on top at the back end of the tanks, or at the back of the footplate. No. 26 was built by Kitson & Co., Leeds (No. 2879), a very popular firm with several South Wales railways, and set the pattern for loco construction for the next twenty years. It had 17½ in. cylinders, 4 ft 6 in. diameter wheels, and worked at 140 psi. It passed into GW hands in 1922 and, after heavy overhaul at Swindon which included GW smokebox arrangement, it was renumbered 163. It returned to Cardiff Docks early in 1926, and remained there until transferred to Cardiff Cathays in October 1930, thence Radyr in March 1931 and finally to Ferndale in June 1931 from which shed it was taken out of service in July 1932. Although placed on the Sales List, it lingered on Swindon Dump until broken up in February 1935.

No. 26 was the last locomotives to be acquired by the Bute Trustees, although two further similar engines, Nos. 27 and 28, delivered the following year, were almost certainly ordered whilst the Trustees were in charge, but delivered after the new company, The Bute Docks Co., was created to manage dock affairs. These two engines were also built by Kitson (Nos. 3068 and 3069), and differed from No. 26 in that they worked at 160 psi and had larger fireboxes. These became GWR Nos. 162 and 159. The first was also withdrawn in July 1932, put on the Sales List, but broken up in February 1935. No. 159 lasted much longer. It was sold direct from Running Stock on 5th February, 1931 to the Lambton, Hetton and Joicey Collieries (via a dealer, R.H. Longbotham) where it became the colliery company's No. 55, and was not cut up until April 1960.

The next two engines acquired were 0–6–0Ts Nos. 29 and 30, also built by Kitson (Works Nos. 3132 and 3133) and delivered in 1889.

They were similar to the 0–6–2Ts, but without a bunker, a plain cab back sheet with spectacle plates only being provided, with the coal once again having to be stocked on the top of the tanks. The principal dimensions were as for the 0–6–2Ts. Both passed into GWR hands becoming Nos. 692 and 691 respectively, and both were sold via Wynne, Jones & Co. of Swansea on 16th March, 1929 direct from Running Stock, becoming Ebbw Vale Iron and Steel Co.'s Nos. 38 *Irthlingborough* and 40 *Cwmcarn* respectively. The latter was scrapped in 1946, but, after the Ebbw Vale Co. was taken over by Richard Thomas and Baldwins Ltd in 1935, No. 38 was transferred to that Company's works at Scunthorpe, where it lasted until January 1957.

The old No. 1 was again renumbered to 31 in 1894, in order to make that number available for a further Kitson built 0–6–2T (Works No. 3580) that was delivered that year. That locomotive was the same as Nos. 27 and 28, and was renumbered 156 by the GWR. It was sent to the makers for overhaul in December 1924, returning to Cardiff Docks in April 1925. It later had spells at both Cardiff Cathays and Radyr before being sold from Running Stock on 5th February, 1931 to Mr R.H. Longbotham, on behalf of the Lambton, Hetton and Joicey Collieries, where it became that company's No. 56 and lasted until 1963.

In 1895 two further Kitson built 0–6–0Ts (Works Nos. 3602 and 3603) were delivered as Bute Nos. 3 and 13. These were practically identical to Nos. 29 and 30 of 1889, and followed the same pattern history. Renumbered 686 and 690 by the GWR, the first was cut up at Swindon in August 1925, but the latter was withdrawn from service in October 1926, placed on the Sales List and was sold in May 1927 via the dealers Wynne Jones & Co., to Guest, Keen and Nettlefolds Ltd, Dowlais Works becoming their No. 16. It lasted until 1948.

By the time the next new engines arrived the dock company had changed its name to the Cardiff Railway Company. The first engine was a small 0–4–0ST No. 5, built by Kitson & Co. (Works No. 3799) to replace the old Manning Wardle 0–4–0ST carrying the same number, which had completed 36 years of hard work around the dock sidings. The new No. 5 had a saddle tank covering both barrel and firebox and an overall cab, but again no bunker, and was fitted with the Hawthorn Kitson valve gear with the link above the running plate. For some years that was protected by a side plate which resembled a tank side, but was removed in later CR days. It passed into GW hands in 1922 and was renumbered 1338. For some years it remained at Cardiff, and was a favourite with local firms who wished to hire an engine when their own was out of action. It had a spell at the Dowlais Works in 1937, at Baldwin's Ltd in 1940 and with South Wales Transport Ltd in 1942. Later that year it was sent to Taunton for working at

Bridgwater Docks, where it remained until June 1960 when it was transferred to Swansea East Dock to assist the local 0–4–0STs in the twilight of steam. It was taken out of service at Swansea on the 30th September 1963 and sold to Mr B. Kinsey on the 23rd April, 1964.

It was then taken to the old Bleadon and Uphill station near Weston-super-Mare for preservation and for some years was a show-piece at the site, but although still there (December 1985) its condition has deteriorated in recent years, with weeds and brambles growing all around it. As by far the most travelled of the former Cardiff Railway engines, the last survivor of that company, and the last standard gauge constituent engine to be withdrawn, it is hoped that it will be restored to its former glory in due course.

Two further 0–6–2Ts, Nos. 9 and 10, were delivered by Kitsons (Nos. 3869 and 3870) later in 1898. They were similar to the others Kitsons had supplied in 1887 and 1894 apart from larger bunkers (with the new railway in mind) and increased wheelbase to match. They became GWR Nos. 157 and 158. The first was overhauled at Swindon in 1923 during which the internal smokebox arrangement was improved to GW pattern, but the only external change was the fitting of a GW pattern chimney and safety valves. It returned to Cardiff Docks from where it was withdrawn in October 1928 and cut up at Swindon in February 1929. No. 158 was overhauled by Messrs Kitson for the GW in May 1925 and also returned to Cardiff Docks. It lasted until May 1932, was placed on the Sales List, and finally cut up in May 1934.

Early in 1899 Kitsons supplied two more 0–6–0Ts, Nos. 4 and 8, which carried Works Nos. 3871 and 3872. They were similar to the other 0–6–0Ts which the firm had supplied in 1895, and in 1922 were added to GWR stock as Nos. 687 and 688. The former had a short GW career being condemned in June 1925 and cut up at Swindon two months later; No. 688 lasted a few years longer as a GW engine and was sold from Running Stock on 20th October, 1931 to Guest Keen and Nettlefolds, Dowlais, via the agents Wynne Jones & Co. It became GKN No. 15 and lasted until August 1950.

Finally, later in 1899, Kitsons delivered a further 0–4–0ST identical to No. 5 supplied the previous year. This was Kitson No. 3969, and Cardiff Rly No. 6. Unlike No. 5 it rarely ventured beyond the confines of Cardiff Docks until GWR days, when it paid a few visits to Caerphilly Works for overhaul. It became GW 1339, and had one lengthy spell away from home when it was on loan to a quarry firm in the Bristol area during most of 1930. It was condemned on 6th May, 1932 at Swindon, and placed on the Sales List. For the next couple of years it could usually be seen coupled to No. 1340 *Trojan*, the Alexandra Dock 0–4–0ST then also on the Sales List but, unlike its partner, it

0–6–2T No. 28 (Kitson 1887) at the docks, *c*.1906. *F. Equeall*

0–6–0T GW No. 691 (CR No. 30) built by Kitson in 1889, at the Rhymney Railway Docks shed, *c*.1926. *Real Photographs*

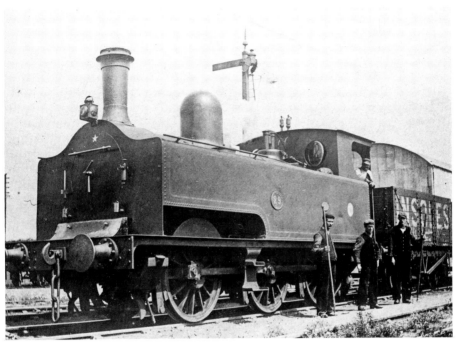

0–6–0T No. 29 (Kitson 1889) also seen at the docks, *c.*1906.   *F. Equeall*

No. 29 became GW No. 692. It was sold in March 1929 to become Ebbw Vale Iron & Steel Co's No. 38 *Irthlingborough*. Photographed on 11th April, 1936.
                                                                      R.G. Jarvis

0–6–2T No. 1 (Kitson 1894), later GW No. 156. *Locomotive Publishing Co.*

The first locomotive delivered to the Cardiff Railway Co. was 0–4–0ST No. 5 (Kitson 1898). She is seen here in original condition at the docks, *c.*1906.

F. Equeall

No. 5 in later CR days, with the side protection panels removed.

Real Photographs

0–6–2T No. 9 (Kitson 1898) at the docks, *c.*1906; she became GW No. 157 and was withdrawn in October 1928.
F. Equeall

0–6–2T No. 158 (CR No. 10) built by Kitson in 1898, at Radyr, *c.*1931.
Author's Collection

0–6–0T No. 688 (CR No. 8) built by Kitson in 1899, seen at East Moors shed on 11th August, 1924.
Real Photographs

0–4–0ST No. 1339 (CR No. 6) alongside the Rhymney Railway Docks shed, c.1926.
Real Photographs

In nearly new condition 0–6–2T No. 11 (Kitson 1905) poses with staff at Tyndall Street Crossing.
F. Equeall

did not find a buyer and was eventually broken up in June 1934.

The next engines were not added until 1905, by which time it appears that the Cardiff authorities felt more confident that their railway would eventually link up with the TVR, requiring powerful 0-6-2Ts to handle the expected volume of coal traffic. That year Kitson supplied two larger engines with full length tanks sloping at the front, with water capacity 2,300 gallons, and a larger bunker holding 3 tons of coal. They carried CR Nos. 11 and 21 (Kitson Nos. 4333 and 4334). These were far from handsome engines, in fact, the forward sloping tanks surrounding the gap in same for maintenance purposes, made them look most ungainly machines. Still, with 18 in. diameter cylinders, 4 ft 6 in. driving wheels and working pressure of 160 psi, they were the most powerful engines on the CR at the time. They passed into GWR stock as GW Nos. 160 and 161. The former was sent to Swindon in 1922 and rebuilt with a domed belpaire boiler (49 GW) which had originally (1911) been fitted at Swindon to Rhondda and Swansea Bay Railway 0-6-2T No. 13 (GW 178) and was later fitted to another RSB 0-6-2T, GW No. 173, in 1930. The Cardiff engine returned to the docks for just over twelve months, but early in 1924 was transferred to Newport Pill for working at Newport Docks, and remained there until taken out of service in April 1930, and cut up at Caerphilly the following month. No. 161 also strayed from its home ground in GWR days, as it worked from Senghenydd from August 1927 until February 1928, afterwards returning to Cardiff Docks from where it was taken out of service on 1st October, 1929, and cut up at Swindon the following month.

With fortunes flagging again late in 1906, the CR returned to the second hand market later that year, and in December purchased three old saddle tanks of the 1661 class from the GWR. These were Nos. 1676 which became CR No. 23, 1689 (25) and 1667 (31). With their 5 ft 2 in. diameter wheels they were hardly the ideal engines for dock work but, being fitted with vacuum brakes they were also used as spare passenger engines for the steam rail car duties, particularly from 1911 to 1914. All three had their boilers rebuilt or replaced in 1922, when the engines resumed their former GWR numbers, after which they were looked on as normal GW stock, not constituent, despite having the usual absorbed type numberplates with the letters GWR between the top rim and the loco number. No. 1689 (CR 25) had been fitted with an all over cab at Tyndall Street, but this was Cardiff Railway pattern, and it was replaced by a standard GW cab when the engine was rebuilt with pannier tanks at Swindon in 1926. It lasted a further five years and was condemned in April 1931 and cut up at Swindon in July 1932. No. 1667 was also fitted with pannier tanks, and a Standard 9 domed boiler, early in 1926. It also did a further five years shunting at the docks, being taken out of service in August 1931 and scrapped at Swindon three months later. The third, No. 1676, was little altered in GW days and remained a saddle tank. It was moved to Swansea (Landore) in March 1925, and thence to Swansea East Dock in April 1926, from which depot it was withdrawn in October and broken up the following month.

We now pass to the ultimate in Cardiff Railway 0–6–2Ts, the three engines of the '33' class, delivered by Kitsons (Nos. 4595 and 4597) in 1908, the Cardiff Railway Nos. being 33 to 35. Despite the hostility between the two companies at the time, these were almost identical to the Taff Vale '04' class, even to the thick ungainly chimney. However, the Cardiff engines had longer forward sloping tanks at the front end, cut away at the underside for ease of maintenance of the inside rods and motion, and were not equipped with the vacuum brakes as were the TVR engines.

They became GWR Nos. 153 to 155, the last numbered being the only ex CR engine to be rebuilt with a Standard GW tapered domeless boiler, at Caerphilly in February 1928. Nos. 153 and 154 were transferred to Barry in December 1928, although No. 153 did not last long and was taken out of service in December 1930, put on the Sales List, and stabled on Swindon Dump until cut up in February 1934. No. 154 lasted until June 1934 and was also put on the Sales List, but found a purchaser quickly. It was sold, via a dealer, R. Frazer of Hebburn, to the Hartley Main Colliery becoming that company's No. 27. At Hebburn the forward sloping tank section was removed in the later 1930s, to give better visibility for the engine crew during shunting operations and, as such, lasted until September 1960.

After rebuilding, No. 155 spent the rest of her days in the Cardiff area, mostly at East Dock shed. It was widely used on valley work, and taking coal trains from the storage sidings to the tip roads. It also was the last CR engine to go up their old main line, being frequently used in the 1948–50 period on trains to Nantgarw Colliery, whilst the modern colliery was being developed. It was finally withdrawn in September 1953 and as a farewell tribute was coupled together at Swindon with a Taff Vale, a Rhymney, and a Brecon and Merthyr 0–6–2T, the old antagonists parading together awaiting their end. No. 155 spent a brief period as Loco Works pilot, but was cut up late in December 1953.

With their hopes dashed of making a commercial success of their main line into the valleys, the only engine purchased in the next ten years was the 2–4–2T *The Earl of Dumfries,* second hand from the LNWR in 1914. It was acquired to act as spare passenger engine when one of the steam cars was out of commission. Little has been written about this engine whilst on the Cardiff Railway, but it did achieve two distinctions. It was the only Cardiff engine known to have carried a name; and secondly, it was the first engine sent to Swindon for scrap after the 1922 amalgamation, being broken up long before it had been allocated its GW number 1327. As Cardiff Railway 36, a number only carried on the buffer beams, it did not distinguish itself on the modest passenger duties and was, to a large extent, displaced in 1919. It was certainly out of use at the Cardiff Railway loco shed at East Moors (Cardiff Docks) for some months before the GWR took over, and was promptly scrapped at Swindon in May 1922.

No more engines were acquired until the Government terms for settlement of their takeover of the railways of Great Britain during World War I were known when, like most other railway companies, the Cardiff burst forth to order modern stock to replace worn out engines, and those sold out of service during the War. Seven further tank engines were ordered, three from Messrs Kitson, and four new pattern 0–6–0STs from Hudswell Clarke & Co.

The Kitson engines arrived in 1919, Nos. 20 and 22 were 0–6–2Ts, Works Nos. 5180 and 5181. These were identical to Nos. 11 and 21 supplied in 1905, apart from being vacuum fitted. The third was an 0–6–0T (Kitson No. 5182) again similar to Nos. 3 and 13 supplied in 1895! This was given CR No. 7 and, although nominally a dock shunter, it took over most of the passenger work. No. 22 also did some passenger work as a relief from its mineral duties.

The 0–6–2Ts were given GW Nos. 151 and 152, but were little altered by their new owners apart from 152 receiving a GW safety valve in place of its Ross Pop valves in August 1926. Both engines were transferred to Barry in September 1928, from which shed No. 151 was taken out of service on the 20th February, 1930 and cut up at Swindon the following month. No. 152 lasted a little longer. It was sent to Caerphilly for overhaul late in 1936, condemned there on the 12th December of that year, but sent to Swindon for cutting up, in February 1937.

The 0–6–0T No. 7 became GWR 685, and was taken off passenger work for the more onerous duties of dock shunting immediately the GWR took control late in March 1922. It continued working in the Cardiff area until sold direct from running stock to the Carlton Collieries Association on 20th October, 1931, working at Carlton Main Colliery, Grimethorpe, as their No. 1 until scrapped in May 1953.

The last engines received by the Cardiff Railway were the four 0–6–0ST built by Hudswell, Clarke & Co. of Leeds (Works Nos. 1404/5/7/8) in 1920. These were very impressive machines, with 18 in. diameter cylinders, 4 ft 1½ in. wheels and worked at 175 psi. The basic design had already been proven as very similar engines were employed by the Powell Duffryn Steam Coal Co., and their efficiency

0–6–0ST No. 1689 (CR No. 25) obtained second hand from the GWR in 1906, at Cardiff Docks shed, *c.*1926.   *Photomatic Ltd*

0–6–0ST No. 31, also ex-GWR in 1906, at the docks January 1920. (Number restored to GW 1667 in 1922).   *Real Photographs*

0–6–2T No. 34 (Kitson 1908) at the docks *c*.1920.   *Real Photographs*

No. 34 became GW No. 154 and was sold in September 1934 to become Hartley Main Collieries' No. 27, seen here at Seaton Delavel, *c*.1938. Note the tanks shortened at the front end to give better visibility to the footplate crews.

L.G. Charlton Collection

0–6–2T 155 (CR No. 35) built by Kitson in 1908, as rebuilt with GW S/3 taper
boiler. Near Cardiff East Dock shed, *c.*1950. *Author's Collection*

2–4–2T No. 36 *The Earl of Dumfries* (ex-LNWR in 1914) under repair at East
Moors Shed, January 1920. *The late W. Beckerlegge*

The Earl of Dumfries at Tyndall Street Yard *c.*1920. *Real Photographs*

0–6–2T No. 151 (CR No. 20) built by Kitson in 1919, at East Moors *c.*1924.
Real Photographs

0–6–0ST No. 32 (Hudswell Clarke 1920) at the docks, *c.*1921. *Real Photographs*

Former 0–6–0ST No. 16, as rebuilt with GW S/11 boiler and pannier tanks. As No. 682 it was photographed at Swindon Locomotive Yard on 10th October, 1953, five days after withdrawal. It was used for several months afterwards as a works pilot. *Author*

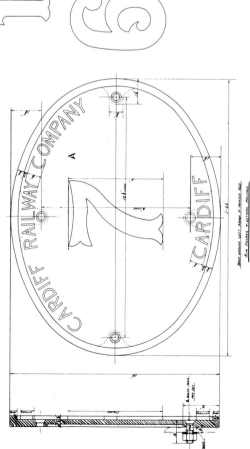

Numberplate of CR 0–6–0T No. 7.
Author's Collection

doubtless impressed the CR's Engineer. They were numbered 14, 16, 17 and 32, the last two were vacuum fitted and did occasional passenger work. However, they proved very fine dock shunters and lasted until 1953–5, although all were rebuilt by the GWR. They became GW Nos. 681–684, in the same order as their CR numbers, No. 683 being rebuilt in October 1926 at Swindon with a Standard 9 domed boiler and pannier tanks. The other three were similarly rebuilt at Caerphilly, when in shops for heavy overhaul, No. 681 in February 1930, No. 684 in December 1936, and No. 682 as late as October 1939. As such they continued to give hard service at the docks until despatched to Swindon, one by one, for withdrawal. All were used for lengthy periods as Loco Works pilots.

No. 681 withdrawn from service 16th February, 1955   Broken up November 1955
No. 682 withdrawn from service 5th October, 1953   Broken up September 1954
No. 683 withdrawn from service 20th December, 1954   Broken up March 1956
No. 684 withdrawn from service 28th May, 1954   Broken up May 1955

Thus ends this outline history of all the engines known to have worked for the Bute Trustees, the Bute Dock Co. and the Cardiff Railway. Generally speaking their engines were austere and robust in design rather than handsome but, apart from some of the earlier locos obtained second hand, were particularly useful for dock shunting and hauling trains of coal for comparatively short distances from storage sidings to tip roads. Only the later 0–6–2Ts were designed with an eye to them bringing coal down from the valleys to the storage sidings, and few of them ever achieved that aim.

In the early days it is said the engines were painted green, but this was changed to unlined black soon after the Bute Dock Co. was formed. That remained the colour for the remainder of the Dock Co., and the Railway Co., although in later years some of the engines were lined out, initially with a broad red line with finer gold supplementary lining, but later with fine white lining replacing the gold. Painted numbers only appeared on the tank sides in the early days, also a motif of the Marquis' coronet. Brass numberplates were used after the Bute Docks Co. was formed, although painted numbers only appeared on the final four 0–6–0STs of 1920. The LNWR 2–4–2T only carried its nameplates and the coat of arms of the Cardiff Railway Co., the number 36 was carried on the buffer beams.

The limited space available at Tyndall Street for stabling locomotives, resulted in a large new six road "straight" shed being opened at East Moors, on the eastern side (southern end) of the East Dock in 1881. This was of ample size to cope with the needs of the company until GW days, the shed being closed on 8th March, 1926, doubtless due to the close proximity of the former Rhymney Railway engine shed at Cardiff Docks. The last named shed was itself demolished in 1930 and the new Cardiff East Dock shed emerged on the site in 1931 and it was at this shed that many of the former CR engines were eventually stabled, along with other dock shunters and valley "coal" engines. Tyndall Street Works, more commonly known as Bute Yard in later years, continued to carry out locomotive repairs for the remainder of CR days, although during the 1914–18 War much of the repair work had to be put out to contract. The GWR closed the yard for locomotive repairs in September 1922, but it remained in use as a dock mechanical engineering workshop for a further ten years, being vacated by the GWR in October 1932.

The first locomotive superintendent was Samuel Allen in 1870, who was previously with Messrs Parfitt and Jenkins, the engineering firm "across the road" from Tyndall Street works, who had supplied the Trustees with their first purpose built heavy dock shunter the previous year. Doubtless Allen had been very much involved in the design and construction of that engine, and as it proved an excellent machine when compared with the motley collection of locomotives already working, it is not surprising that he was invited to take charge of the Marquis' loco stock and plan future construction.

When Allen retired in 1881 there was a standardised class of 13 Parfitt and Jenkins shunters performing all major work at the docks (apart from the specialised light duties of the 0–4–0STs), and a large, first rate, engine shed at East Moors where the fleet could be stabled and receive their day-to-day maintenance. With this in mind the Trustees decided not to renew the post and locomotives came under the responsibility of the existing Chief Engineer, John McConnochie. He also retired the following year but it was during his brief period in charge of locomotives that he reverted to the old policy of purchasing second hand, and acquired the North London Railway 4–4–0Ts. He was followed by Charles L. Hunter who died in 1902, having, in that comparatively short period of time, served the Trustees, the Bute Docks Company and finally the Cardiff Railway Co. He was responsible for bringing more modern and more powerful locomotives (particularly the 0–6–2Ts) to the docks to cope with the massive increase in the steam coal export trade during his period in office. He was also responsible for "weeding out" many of the older and less useful engines in his charge, and rebuilding the others at Tyndall Street.

After Hunter's death, Mr H.S.C. Ree took over, in most respects following Hunter's policy, but also delving into the second-hand market on occasions. Alaric Hope took over in 1914 following Ree's retirement, and remained in charge until amalgamation with the GWR in 1922.

Although locomotive design at the docks generally followed the current practice, two detail differences appeared during the Hunter

GW 0–4–2T No. 1421 with domeless boiler and bunker weatherboard, at Cathays shed on 9th August, 1924. It was regularly used in this condition on the CR passenger services during 1923 and 1924.   *The late W. Beckerlegge*

0–6–2T No. 511 (formerly TVR 'M1' class No. 74) which did several spells on the CR passenger services 1925–1929.   *Real Photographs*

The Cardiff Railway engine shed at East Moors *c.*1920. (Viewed from the south end). *Locomotive Publishing Co.*

LNWR 'Coal Tank' 0–6–2T No. 3739, and former RR 2–4–2ST No. 1324, rest in the yard at Cardiff Docks engine shed, 7th August, 1924. *Lens of Sutton*

The last steam dock shunters, 0–6–0PTs Nos. 6701, 6702, 6744 and 6751, at Cardiff East Dock shed, 16th March, 1958, prior to replacement by diesel shunters. *A. Manship*

No. 1421 stands alongside the Rhymney Railway Docks shed, *c.* August 1922. *Locomotive Publishing Co.*

period that are instantly recognisable by students of locomotive history, the design of the chimney and cabs of many of the engines rebuilt at Tyndall Street. The shape of the cab sheeting, particularly that for the fixing of the bunker support, had a distinctly foreign look about it, whilst the chimney design was peculiar to Cardiff Railway and its predecessor. Many of the engines never had these features, particularly the more modern 0–6–0Ts and 0–6–2Ts, but several of the older engines, especially those from Parfitt and Jenkins, were thus altered. A number of the earlier engines originally had stovepipe chimneys, but those that survived received the "Hunter" type when rebuilt.

The CR did not record locomotive mileages, but the GWR did so for constituent companies as from 20th May, 1922. The four Hudswell Clarke 1920 0–6–0STs each easily achieved over 500,000 miles: 681 (14) with 607,497; 682 (16) 533,209; 683 (17) 586,565 and 684 (32) with 580,770.

The last surviving 0–6–2T 155 (35) recorded 445,778 miles, whilst the diminutive 0–4–0ST 1338 (No. 5) totalled 353,985 miles between May 1922 and September 1963.

Initially dock shunting was performed by any suitable Cardiff Railway engine, particularly the Parfitt and Jenkins 0–6–0STs and their modern side tank counterparts, although there was sufficient "sharp curve" wharf work to keep the two 0–4–0STs employed. The 0–6–2Ts were used on heavier work, particularly moving coal trains from storage sidings to tip roads. Both the RR and TVR also maintained a few locos for dock shunting.

After the GWR took over, a wide variety of absorbed locos worked within the docks along with a few of their own small wheeled pannier tanks. As the older CR engines were withdrawn, they were mainly replaced by Barry Railway 'F' class 0–6–0STs (many rebuilt as PTs by the GW), a class most suitable for heavy dock shunting, as were the Rhymney 'S' class 0–6–0Ts, the latter had been used at the docks prior to the amalgamation, of course.

When the CR East Moors shed was closed in 1926, most of its locos were transferred to the nearby Docks shed of the RR, which accommodated passenger engines (RR section) and main line mineral engines, as well as the dock shunters. By 1928 all the passenger workings had been transferred to the former TVR shed at Cardiff Cathays, after which the Docks shed was responsible for all dock workings, along with goods and mineral workings in the Rhymney Valley and on the former CR line.

A visit paid to the Docks shed on Whit Sunday, 31st March 1929, revealed a wide selection of absorbed engines. Of a grand total of 68 engines present, only seven were from the GWR. The full list comprised:

CR	0–6–2Ts	156, 158, 159, 161, 162	
	0–6–0T	681, 682, 684, 685, also 1667 (ex GWR)	
	0–4–0T	1339	*11 CR*
RR	0–6–2T	A/A1 class, 52, 57, 59, 60, 63, 64, 66, 67, 69, 70, 71, 73	
	"	R class, 38	
	0–6–0T	S/S1 class, 604, 605, 606, 609, 610, 611	*19 RR*
TVR	0–6–2T	344, 366 (A class), 278, 294, 311 (04 class), 446 (0 class), 433 (03 class)	*7 TVR*
Barry	0–6–0T	702 (A class), 781, 783 (E Class)	
		F class, 706, 708, 711, 712, 713, 714, 716, 717, 719, 720, 723, 724, 725, 729, 742, 754, 776, 778, 780, 807	*23 BR*
ADR	0–4–0T	1340 *Trojan*	*1 ADR*
GWR	0–6–2T	5615	
	0–6–0T	1272, 1928, 1970, 2000, 2022, 2086	*7 GWR*
			Total *68*

Early the following year the Docks shed was demolished and a new shed, Cardiff East Dock, built on the site, officially opened 19th January, 1931. During the construction period the GWR introduced the 67XX class, identical to the 57XX 0–6–0 pannier tanks apart from the omission of vacuum brakes, and the first ten engines, 6700–6709 were sent new to Cardiff East Dock, and all remained there throughout the shed's initial history as a steam shed, apart from 6700 which was transferred to the Swansea area a few months before closure to steam as from 8th March 1958. Arrival of Nos. 6700–6709 meant the departure of older 0–6–0Ts from CED, particularly of the Barry 'F' class.

In 1947 the GW introduced a new version of the 67XX class. Numbered 6751 upwards they were fitted with the improved style of cab, already fitted to all other modern GW 0–6–0PTs from 1933 onwards. Of the new batch Nos. 6751/65/67/70/71/73/78 and 79 were all sent new to CED and remained there until (or almost until) closure to steam dock shunters.

By the time 6779 was delivered in December 1950 a start had been made of withdrawing the more modern absorbed 0–6–0Ts and 0–6–2Ts and by the late summer of 1955 all had gone from CED.

Surprisingly there were still sufficient duties at the shed for BR(WR) to send down a further batch of ten new pannier tanks, Nos. 3400–3409, these being delivered to CED between December 1955 and September 1956. These were of Hawksworth's design, No. 3409 having the distinction of being the last engine of GWR design to be built. Their stay at CED was fairly brief, 350 HP shunters started work at the dock the following year, and with the closure of CED to steam Nos. 3400–3409 were transferred to Radyr (at the north end of Cardiff) from where they were used on mineral and goods workings to the valleys, and also on the Whitchurch goods on the Coryton branch.

Although not strictly part of this story, Cardiff East Dock shed re-opened to steam on 10th September, 1962 to maintain main line steam locos following the closure of Cardiff Canton shed for rebuilding as a diesel servicing and maintenance depot. Before it finally closed for the last time, on 2nd August, 1965, it was host to many famous engines, particularly 92220 *Evening Star* (shedded at CED) and 7029 *Clun Castle* (a regular visitor from Gloucester).

ROLLING STOCK

The first carriage stock vehicle, which arrived in 1899, was a small four wheeled Inspection Car, and was almost certainly acquired second-hand. Little is known about it, as it does not appear to have merited being detailed in any CR records the author has seen, but its main use would appear to have been to convey officials around the dock area, or for inspection trips to the main line during construction. As can be seen from the illustration, it was a very modest vehicle, with a short central body with bench type seating each side, and a verandah at each end, one of which housed a screw-down brake. The lower panels of the body were adorned with the company's Coat of Arms towards each end of the passenger compartment, with the vehicle's running number (1) at the extreme ends. It disappeared from the stock list in 1920, presumably sold for scrap as, by that time, alternative coaching stock was available for inspection purposes.

It was not until 1911 that the first public passenger carrying vehicles arrived, the two steam rail cars and their trailers already mentioned, along with a spare engine unit. The latter was numbered 1 in a motor engine list, whilst the two rail cars became Nos. 2 and 3, and the trailers Nos. 4 and 5, in the carriage stock list. No. 2 car was delivered on 23rd February, 1911, had a successful trial trip on the new line on 27th February, and initiated the public service on Wednesday, 1st March. The other cars arrived at Cardiff a few days later.

Both steam cars and trailers bore a very marked resemblance to GWR cars of the period and initially were painted GWR colours, although later witnesses have said the lower panels were more lake than chocolate, and the upper panels white, suggesting a slight move towards LNWR colouring may have taken place over the years. The steam cars could be driven from either end, the main driving cab having a small vertical boiler similar to GWR cars. The cars themselves were constructed by the Gloucester C&W Co., the engine bogies by Messrs W. Sisson & Co. Ltd, also of Gloucester, and the boilers by Messrs Abbot & Co. Ltd of Newark on Trent. The drive was on the rear pair of wheels of the engine bogie, which were 4 ft in diameter, the front carrying wheels were of 3 ft 7 in. diameter. Working pressure was 160 psi, water capacity 500 gallons, and 10 cwt of coal could be carried. The wheelbase was 8 ft + 30 ft + 8 ft and the length over buffers 68 ft 11¼ in. The cars had a small first class compartment seating 16 people, and a large open third class seating 48, a total of 64, and the vestibule was fitted with retractable steps for serving the halts not provided with platforms. The trailer cars were of a similar outward appearance; they had three third class passenger compartments seating 16 + 40 + 24, a total of 80. The trailers had a driving compartment at one end, but were not gangwayed at the opposite end for through communication with the rail cars.

One rail car with trailer sufficed for the sparse passenger traffic, even one trailer hauled by a vacuum fitted loco was often used at off-peak periods. The Cardiff Railway had been very late on the scene in the steam rail car era, most of the larger railways having already gone over to Auto train working, with the cars gradually being phased out and converted to trailers with a driving compartment at one end, and worked as one or two car units with an ordinary small engine converted for auto working.

Hence, when the Cardiff cars needed heavy overhaul in 1919, the opportunity was taken to convert the two steam cars to trailers and, with the existing trailers, make up two gangwayed pairs. The engine bogies and main driving compartment was removed from the steam cars, and replaced by a normal carriage bogie, and a small passenger compartment with end vestibule and gangway. As rebuilt, by the makers at Gloucester, late 1919/early 1920, the rebuilt cars resembled the original trailers 4 and 5, and the seating was increased to 80 per car as below:

Car 2   16 (Firsts) + 32 (Thirds) + 32 (Thirds)
Car 3   16 (Firsts) + 32 (Thirds) + 16 (Thirds – non-smoking)
                                    + 16 (Thirds – smoking)

As returned from Gloucester the four trailers were formed into two pairs – Cars 2 and 5, and Cars 3 and 4. Although fitted for auto

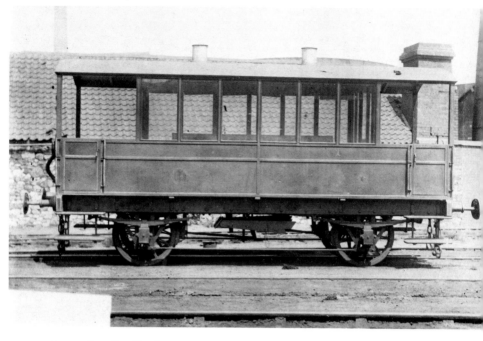

Inspection Car No. 1, *c*.1920.

Real Photographs

Steam Rail Motor No. 3 seen here at the maker's works, February 1911.
Gloucester C. & W. Co.

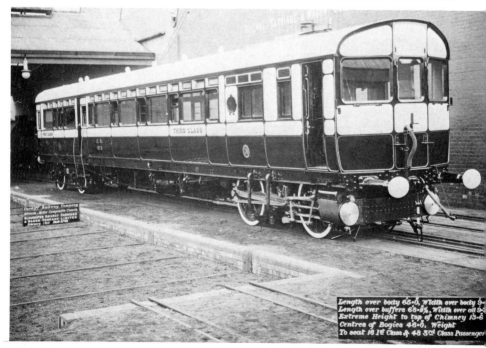

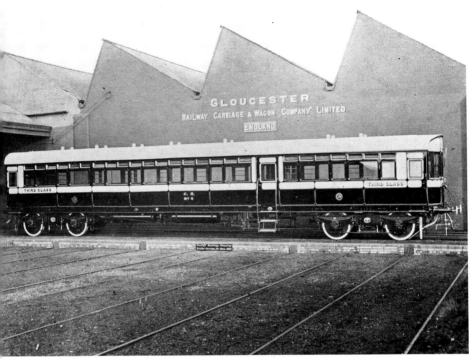

Trailer No. 4 at the maker's works, November 1910. *Gloucester C & W Co.*

Auto trailers Nos. 143 (CR 3) and 144 (CR 4) at Caerphilly Factory on 28th May, 1957, shortly after withdrawal. *Author*

Four wheel Compo Brake, as running on the Bishops Castle Railway (latterly GW Brake Third No. 4347, before that CR No. 8, and originally a Hull & Barnsley five compartment Third). *Lens of Sutton*

Mineral brake van No. 1971, passing through the former RR Cardiff Parade Station; Locomotive 0–6–2T GW No. 160 (CR 11), 4th April, 1923.

Author's Collection

Covered van No. 1967, built by Gloucester C&W Co., 1910.

Gloucester C&W Co.

Six plank open docks wagon No. 403 on Swindon Dump, 20th July, 1925.

British Rail

working, they were never used as such in Cardiff Railway days, in fact there is no record that any CR locomotive was ever auto fitted. Before describing their later history, the carriages purchased to replace them whilst they were at Gloucester must be described.

With the rebuilding of the cars in mind, the Cardiff purchased four old carriages from the Hull and Barnsley Railway in April 1919. These were four wheeled Thirds, with a body length of 27 ft 1 in. and which had been constructed for the H&BR by the Metropolitan Railway, C&W Co. in 1885, and were Nos. 3, 11,15 and 16 in that railway company's stock list. They were sold to the Cardiff Railway for £100 each. Two of them (numbers not known), had one end compartment altered to a guard's compartment with brake, and were numbered 7 and 8 in the Cardiff list. The other two were not altered and ran as Cardiff Nos. 6 and 9. The exterior of the vehicles was varnished teak. They normally worked in pairs, Nos. 6 and 7 as one pair, and 8 and 9 as the other. As such they were used for the Cardiff Railway passenger service from late Summer 1919 until the Summer timetable for 1920. Afterwards they were mainly used as workmen's carriages, being attached to the trailer cars as required. With the development of Nantgarw colliery at the time most trains were booked to convey workmen.

Hence when the GWR took control in the Spring of 1922, the company possessed eight coaching stock vehicles, the four trailer cars, and four ex H&B carriages. At least one of the steam rail car engine bogies was still on hand at Cardiff, and this was cut up at Swindon about June 1922.

Although, as detailed in the passenger train services section, the motive power was changed almost immediately, the Cardiff coaching stock vehicles continued to be used for the traffic for most of the remainder of 1922, but late that year Nos. 2 and 5 were sent to the Rhymney Railway factory at Caerphilly for overhaul, whilst the other pair were sent to the former TVR carriage works at Cathays after the return of Nos. 2 and 5 from Caerphilly during 1923. It is not thought that any major alterations were made to any of the cars at either Caerphilly or Cathays, although they were renumbered GW 142–5 (in the same order as the Cardiff numbers). They returned to the Cardiff section singly, and for a year or so were paired with any one of the oddest selection of coaching stock vehicles that were drafted in from neighbouring sections to work the line. One of the first was former Alexandra Dock car GW No. 64, a former Barnum and Bailey Circus coach, on its return from overhaul at Swindon in May 1923, followed by Nos. 90 and 95 conversions from the AD steam rail cars, also after visits to Swindon late Summer 1923 (No. 90) and early 1924 (No. 95).

The Taff Vale section also contributed a few "odds", including one of the lightweight six wheels trailer cars, specially constructed to work with that company's steam rail cars, plus a couple of cars which had been rebuilt from the smaller TVR cars, these without the unsightly overhead wires and pulleys that were a feature of Taff auto cars. The Rhymney section provided one or two of their bogie open thirds, whilst the Barry section occasionally provided their pair of trailers, conversions from steam rail cars. This assortment of vehicles worked in odd pairs sometimes with, and sometimes without, a Cardiff trailer, but all trains during this period, say 1923–5 or possibly 1926 were worked "non auto", whether the vehicles were auto-fitted or not. About 1926 the Cardiff cars were sent to Swindon for fitting up with the GWR system of auto control, and on their return once again worked the Cardiff section as pairs, Nos. 142 + 145 and 143 + 144, pairings which seemed to persist throughout their history.

Meanwhile the former Hull and Barnsley carriages were still used as workmen's vehicles during 1923 and 1924. Nos. 8 and 9 were sent to Swindon for overhaul early in 1923, returning as GWR Nos. 4347 and 4348, after which they worked as single workmen's units, on the Rhymney section as well as the Cardiff. Nos. 6 and 7 were not renumbered (4345 and 4346) until they were repaired at Cardiff Cathays in May 1925. However, with the early decline of Nantgarw Colliery, and ample workmen's coaches available on the Rhymney and Taff Vale sections, they did not last long. The first to go was No. 4347 which was sold to the Bishops Castle Railway in Shropshire on 12th July, 1924, where it was used as a Brake Tri-Composite and survived along with two other South Wales "relics", until the closure of that railway in 1935. No. 4348 lasted a further nine months, being taken out of service period ending 18th April, 1925. The other pair, 4345 and 4346 lasted until late 1926, being withdrawn period ending 25th December of that year.

With such an odd assortment of vehicles being used on the Cardiff section it is not surprising that, as from the Summer timetable of 1923, the service was labelled "One Class only". Certainly most of the cars used were already third class only, and the Cardiff composite cars must either have been downrated, or used as "thirds only" when employed on the Cardiff section.

Until the cut back to Coryton in 1931 most trains on the section consisted of two "non auto" vehicles, usually fairly modern bogie coaches from the TVR and Rhymney sections. All the "relics" had gone by late 1926, the only link being that a pair of TVR steam rail car conversions continued to put in an appearance and did so, in fact, until about 1950. Whilst the majority of the trains were "non auto" with the loco running around at Cardiff and at Rhydyfelin, the Cardiff pairs were often used as auto sets, with either GW auto-fitted pannier tanks or, more frequently, with rebuilt ex TVR 'M1' class 0–6–2Ts which had been fitted with GW auto gear at Swindon when rebuilt. The ex Barry Railway gangwayed auto set (GWR 4303 and 6131) was also used occasionally for the evening service and, once again, the composite vehicle (6131) must have been used temporarily as "third only" for this work.

After the 1931 cut back and the loop had been put in at Coryton, two distinct trains were formed to work the peak traffic, with auto trains covering off-peak periods, particularly in the evenings. The two trains each consisted of five vehicles:

One train –   Three ex TVR Craven built 1921 bogie stock, along with two ex Rhymney bogie open saloons

Second train – Again three ex TVR Craven built 1921 bogie stock, along with two bogie cars, conversions from TVR steam rail cars.

These trains with minor variations, continued to work the Coryton branch for the next 20 years, whilst the auto sets used were the ex-Cardiff pairs, standard GWR auto cars and, occasionally ex-Rhymney auto sets, and the ex-Barry set. From about 1931–5 the regular evening service consisted of one auto car only, GW No. 22, which was propelled up to Coryton, and hauled back to Cardiff with the engine running bunker first.

Traffic remained high until the 1950s when the vast increase in traffic on the roads led to a sharp decrease by rail, and auto sets sufficed for most of what was left on the Coryton branch. Even so five coach trains (by that time mainly comprising GWR standard suburban stock) could still be seen on the branch, particularly for football or rugby excursions on Saturdays.

In June 1958, three car suburban sets took over most of the services, although it was not until the early 1960s that steam finally gave way, and the necessity for the run around loop at Coryton was removed (October 1964). Despite the branch being singled in 1966 and the service severely cut back initially, it is now steadily improving (1985) with the three car diesel sets reigning supreme, and it has even been announced that the new three car diesel "Sprinter" sets will be operating on all the local valley routes by the Summer of 1987.

Turning to wagon stock the vast majority of vehicles owned by the Cardiff Railway were internal user wagons for Docks use only, and were not permitted to work outside the dock area. These wagons were not included in the Ministry of Transport Returns but, fortunately were numbered in the ordinary CR wagon stock list, and

Two plank open docks wagon No. 1227 on Swindon Dump, 20th July, 1925.

British Rail

Twin timber trucks Nos. 1800 and 1801 at maker's works, November 1899.

Gloucester C&W Co.

Former TVR non auto observation trailer, used on the Cardiff Railway line in 1923 and 1924. *C.C. Green*

Former TVR auto trailers Nos. 2506 (TV 353) driving, and 6422 (TV 79) non driving, at Caerphilly Factory, 26th August, 1954. These large auto sets (the TVR had three pairs) were regularly used on the Coryton branch until the advent of the DMUs. *Author*

TVR ten compartment Third No. W2517W (TV 364) at Cardiff General, 23rd March, 1957. These Craven built (1921) carriages were regularly used in Coryton branch trains until *c*.1950. *R.O. Tuck*

RR bogie open Third No. 1067 (RR 41), another type of carriage in regular use on the Coryton branch, *c*.1931–1950. Seen at Caerphilly Factory, 11th July, 1957. *Author*

Barry Railway Trailer No. 4303 (BR 178), used on the Coryton branch in the 1930s. Photographed at Bridgend 1951. *L&GRP, Courtesy David & Charles*

CR "Fasten the Gate" notice at Rhiwbina Halt, 3rd August, 1964. *M. Hale*

recorded in their register in the same way as wagons used on the main line. Unfortunately, like most CR records, the register gave sparse details of the wagons themselves, merely the running number, type and barest details. However, even that is better than nothing at all.

Returning to the official totals, only 43 goods train vehicles are shown at 31st December, 1921, the last return prior to the amalgamation. All passed into GWR hands and were allotted GW running numbers as below:

30–10 ton open wagons with side doors CR Nos. 1950–9 and 1973–92.
  These were allotted GW numbers, 34222/4–7/9/30/1/3/7, 34179/80/2–5/8/9/91/3–6/9, 34202/6/7/10/6/21.
  These were all withdrawn between February 1923 and November 1934. Nos.1950/1/5/7 and 1991 were scrapped still carrying CR numbers.

10–8 ton covered goods vans, CR Nos. 1960–9. Renumbered GW 100773–100782.
  Withdrawn between December 1927 and July 1932.

3 Goods brake vans, CR Nos. 1970, 1971, 1972. Renumbered GWR 10094, 10097, 10104. Condemned March 1926, August 1926, March 1926.

Having disposed of the main line wagon stock (or Common User Wagons as the Cardiff described them) we now turn to what is known of the dock wagons. A list dated 23rd November, 1921 gives a total of 1204 such wagons, plus a further 15 miscellaneous service wagons also solely used within the dock area.

Dealing with the 1204 dock wagons first, these comprised:

399 Coal Wagons, all 10T except CR No. 1514–8T.
731 10T open goods wagons, which included 196 very low sided wagons used for timber and a further 175 with slightly higher sides used both for timber and as open wagons.
44 8T timber trucks, close coupled to form 22 twin sets.
30 8T ballast wagons, used by the PW Dept.

These vehicles were never included in the GW running stock list of wagons, and retained their CR numbers until scrapped or otherwise disposed of. On some the GW prefixed the painted wagon number with the initials CD (Cardiff Docks). They also painted a large white cross on the wagon sides, the standard GW practice to denote internal user wagons.

The twin timber sets were in two series, Nos. 49˚to 72, which had been purchased second-hand from Messrs Andrews and Baby (a local dealer?) forming twelve sets, of which each set was formed of successive numbers, i.e. 49 + 50, 51 + 52 etc. All had been taken out of service by January 1926. The other ten sets were constructed by the

Gloucester C&W Co. in 1899 and carried numbers 1800 to 1819. Once again they were paired in successive numbers form i.e. 1800 + 1801 etc. They were condemned in pairs intermittently between August 1923 and January 1929.

The PW ballast wagons were numbered 1603–1632 and all but three were sold out of stock, again to Messrs Andrews and Baby, as early as 29th June, 1922. The other three, Nos. 1614/5/20, lasted until June 1925, December 1925 and March 1926 respectively.

The varied selection of high and low sided open wagons that were used for coal, timber and general goods were mostly condemned in the 1920s, although a few survived until 3 or 4 years later. Once again several were sold in the early 1920s to Messrs Andrews and Baby, and more to another dealer, the Cymric Trading Co., in the later 1920s. A few low sided open wagons were transferred to Newport Docks in October 1929 but returned to Cardiff Docks in June 1930. The solitary 8 ton coal wagon actually got to Swindon Works, where it was condemned during the period ending 21st February, 1925.

The 15 miscellaneous service vehicles were a mixed bag and comprised:

6 un-numbered open flats without springs – what these were for can only be left to the imagination. Of these, two were broken up shortly after the amalgamation with the GWR, and the other four sold to Messrs Andrews and Baby.
1 flat wagon for carrying a salvage pump.
1 pneumatic plant van.
1 pumping plant van.
1 breakdown van.

Five others carried CR numbers as below:

9 and 10 – 10 ton open wagons for general Engineering Dept use.
No. 634 – Shunting truck.
No. 934 – Protection wagon for PW Dept steam crane.
No. 1301 – Weighbridge Workshop van.

The last survivor of this mixed bag of vehicles was the breakdown van which was condemned at Swindon period ending 24th September, 1932.

Still another official list states that 700 wagons were hired to the Cardiff Railway, comprising 443 open wagons, 233 mineral wagons and 24 special wagons. No trace has been found of these in either the CR or GWR wagon lists, and one can only assume that they were returned to their owners prior to the amalgamation.

Standard GWR wagons and brake vans soon replaced CR vehicles on the main line, and few of the numerous dock wagons survived into the 1930s. Fortunately the official GWR photographer photographed some of the dock wagons on the Dump at Swindon in the mid 1920s, and they will be reproduced with this history, as they show the differing styles of Cardiff Railway marking, and the additional GW marking following the amalgamation.

TRAIN SERVICES

Passenger

When the passenger service was being planned by Col Denniss early in 1910, he was still confident that either amalgamation or a close working relationship between the TV and Cardiff Railway companies was reasonably certain, hence he arranged that the four main stations on the line (Whitchurch, Tongwynlais, Glan-y-llyn and Upper Boat) should have platforms 450 ft long to accommodate the expected Taff Vale trains from the valleys and Pontypridd which would be diverted over the Cardiff line via Treforest Jn. The Taff themselves had proposed such a service during the run up to the 1909 Amalgamation Bill between the companies, with up to 50 per cent of the Taff passenger trains between Cardiff and Pontypridd running via the Cardiff Railway, the remainder using their own main line via Taffs Well.

Several halts were planned along the new line, and it is not clear whether the original plan was for Taff Vale steam rail cars or auto trains to work that service as well between Pontypridd and Cardiff, or whether the Cardiff Railway expected to get running powers into Queen Street (TVR) station at the south, and from Treforest Jn to Pontypridd at the northern end, and work the service with steam rail cars themselves. Both schemes would have necessitated putting in a scissors crossing at Crockherbtown Jn (just north of Queen Street station) to enable CR trains to get into the Taff station, a move widely expected in 1909/10 but which was not achieved until put in by the GWR in 1928.

After the failure and withdrawal of the 1910 Amalgamation Bill the Taff withdrew from such proposals, leaving the Cardiff with four big stations under construction, and a passenger line which would start and finish at halts, with a minimal traffic potential in between. It was decided to go ahead with the steam rail car proposal, and two such cars and two trailers were ordered from the Gloucester C&W Co., to run a modest service between the Rhymney Railway's Parade station at Cardiff and the halt at the northern end of the line at Rhydyfelin. There were no less than five halts and the four stations on the 9¼ miles of CR main line mileage. Two further halts had been planned, but suspended for the time being. As recorded elsewhere in the story, a service of eleven cars each way on weekdays and five

0–6–0T No. 7 leaving Heath Halt on the 2.30 pm Cardiff RR to Rhydyfelin,
17th May, 1919.   *Locomotive Club of Great Britain*

0–6–0T No. 7 on a down passenger train standing at Upper Boat Station in
1920. Note the additional coal supply on the tank top.

G.H.W. Clifford, Courtesy C.C. Green

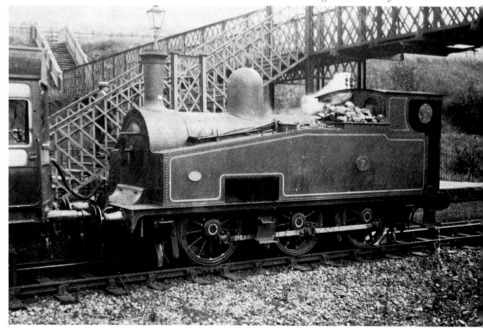

0–6–2T No. 20 heads a coal train for the docks over Tyndall Street bridge, 27th July, 1922.   *R.K. Cope, Courtesy Roger Carpenter*

0–6–2T No. 35 banks a coal train for the docks over Tyndall Street bridge, 27th July, 1922.   *R.K. Cope, Courtesy Roger Carpenter*

0–6–2T GW No. 159 (CR 28) heads a train of freshly limed cattle wagons near Roath Storage Sidings, c.1923. *Welsh Industrial and Maritime Museum, Cardiff*

TVR 'A' class 0–6–2T No. 391 leaving Heath Halt for Coryton on 2nd April, 1951. (The train comprises TVR ten compartment Third, GWR Brake Third, TVR open Third (ex-steam car rebuild), and another TVR ten compartment Third.) *Ian Wright*

each way on Sundays was provided, but even this modest service lost money and it was drastically pruned the following year, although after a few months was partially restored to eight cars each way on weekdays and four on Sundays. With very slight variations that remained the pattern of services until 1920, by which time the steam cars had been converted to trailer cars, and four extra carriages had been acquired. Hence that year the service was increased to ten each way on weekdays. In the final few months prior to the 1922 amalgamation with the GWR a further train each way was added, but from the very first timetable issued by the GWR covering the line (July 1922), the beginnings of the future pattern began to emerge. Eight trains were booked throughout the line (of which five up and six down carried workmen), with one extra on Saturdays but the forerunner of the present Coryton service was established with one morning and one evening train covering the northern outskirts of Cardiff only, and terminating at Whitchurch station.

However, before recording the later changes introduced by the GWR, the motive power in Cardiff days should be detailed. Until 1919, the steam rail cars worked the traffic and when unavailable because of repair, washouts, etc., a vacuum fitted loco – normally one of the three purchased second hand from the GWR in 1906 – worked with one, or both, of the trailer cars. However, in 1914, an LNWR 2–4–2T, No. 1181, was purchased as the spare passenger engine. It was named *The Earl of Dumfries* (another title of the Marquis of Bute) and given the number 36 in the Cardiff list, although there is no evidence that the number was ever carried on the tank sides or bunker. In later Cardiff Railway days *The Earl* became somewhat unreliable, prone to breaking down in outlandish places at the northern end of the line, hence, when a new dock loco (No. 7) was purchased in 1919, it was equipped with the vacuum brake and facilities to carry extra coal on the tanks in front of the cab. This 0–6–0T was the mainstay of the passenger motive power for the next twelve to eighteen months, especially whilst the steam rail cars were at Gloucester for conversion to trailer cars. In 1920 four new powerful 0–6–0STs were obtained from Messrs Hudswell Clarke & Co., and the last two of these (Nos. 17 and 32) were also vacuum fitted for use on the passenger service as required. Nos. 7, 17 and 32 were easily able to cope with the service, and it appears that *The Earl* did little passenger work after the Summer of 1920, and spent long periods at East Moors shed acting as shed pilot or on other menial work. After a further breakdown it was laid aside at shed, and when the GWR took over it was immediately despatched to Swindon (in May 1922) and broken up before the month was out, achieving the unenviable reputation of being the first constituent engine to be cut up following the amalgamation.

Immediately the GW took control they took the three modern Cardiff Railway locos off passenger work and put them on the coal/dock duties for which they had been designed. To replace them three very old double framed 'J' class 0–6–0STs, Nos. 48, 50 and 54, were transferred from the Rhymney section to the Cardiff line. This was early in April 1922, and their performance does not appear to have been much of an improvement on *The Earl*, as all three were shown as having broken down on the line in the first month or so, No. 48 as early as 7th April, 1922. However, the GW persisted with these three, as they were the only vacuum fitted 0–6–0STs on the Rhymney. Occasionally an old GWR 0–6–0ST would be called in when more than one of the Rhymney engines was out of action.

In August 1922 the GW sent one of their own 0–4–2Ts, No. 1421, to work on the line following overhaul at Swindon Works. This much rebuilt 1877 engine was unusual as it was fitted with a domeless boiler at the time, a standard GW safety valve occupying the normal dome position on the boiler. The bunker was also fitted with a tall protective back-plate, with spectacle plates, which must have been more than welcome when running down from Rhydyfelin, with the incessant south west winds and rains which plague the South Wales valleys meeting the bunker-first engine almost head on. However, even that meagre protection was hardly sufficient, and 1421 was taken off the Cardiff passenger service in November 1922. But it was a useful engine for the job, and it returned again for a spell in the late Summer and Autumn of 1923, and for a third spell in 1924, although on that occasion it started in the Spring.

During 1923 a further assortment of oddities worked the passenger service, matching the trailer car curiosities which the GW had transferred to the Cardiff line and which have been described in the carriage notes. In February ex-R&SB 2–4–2T GWR No. 1310 became a regular. This locomotive had been rebuilt with a Swindon tapered boiler late the previous year, also a high roofed cab, but its appearance was spoiled by the bunker side plates which tapered back from the cab end to the back plate. All in all it looked an ungainly engine, but was probably more than useful in the winter months as it had an overall cab to protect the crew from the weather.

Ex-TVR engines began to filter on the line as well. The first were the 4–4–0Ts with very thick chimneys and overhead wires and pulleys for auto gear (Taff Vale style). It is not certain if all three appeared on the line, but at least two did. These engines were not worked as auto whilst on the Cardiff Railway section, in fact there is no record that their auto cars were used with them. A further ex-Taff Vale engine

CR train at Rhydyfelin terminus 1920. Former GWR 0–6–0ST No. 23, with (*Left to Right*) Tom Meyrick, guard, Lily Jenkins, conductress, and Bill Street, passenger train driver. *John White Collection*

used on the line that year was 'M' class 0–6–2T GWR No. 511, which was also TVR auto-fitted. All these Taff engines had overall cabs, hence were probably preferred to the occasional GWR 0–6–0ST sent to help out, as these invariably had open cabs, with only the tarpaulin sheet for weather protection.

The year 1924 saw further ex-TVR locos on the passenger work. These were one or two of the more handsome 4–4–2Ts of the Taff 'C' class. Although also auto-fitted TVR style they were a nicely proportioned engine in comparison with most of the museum pieces the GWR had transferred from neighbouring sections to work the line. Although no records have been traced it would appear that No. 1301 was most likely to have been the first to appear on the Cardiff line, and that Nos. 1304 and 1305 are likely to have had spells in both 1924 and 1925. During the latter year another odd couple were sent up from Barry, 'C' class 2–4–2Ts Nos. 1322 and 1323, the former rebuilt with GW domed boiler and high roofed cab, the latter still mainly in Barry Railway condition. Both spent considerable periods on the Cardiff section in 1925.

By 1926, the oddities had mostly vanished or been consigned to the scrap yard, and GW No. 511 – by now fitted with GW auto gear – reappeared on the line. GW 0–6–0STs were more frequent, whilst on occasions the new '5600' class 0–6–2Ts were used on the passenger service. Further 'M1' class 0–6–2Ts appeared in 1927, these had been rebuilt with GW domed boilers, cabs and bunkers and fitted with GW auto gear. Nos. 583 and 584 came in 1927 followed by Nos. 506 and 573 in 1928, and all were regulars on the line, along with GWR 0–6–0STs or PTs until the line was cut back to Coryton in 1931.

Before proceeding to that period, it is interesting to see how the GWR developed the North Cardiff suburban service during the 1920s, whilst still maintaining a more than adequate service for the northern end of the line. Despite the massive drop in traffic during the depression years which followed the General Strike of 1926, the weekday service remained eight each way, with one extra on Saturdays until the closure north of Coryton in 1931. To illustrate the problem the GW faced, receipts at Tongwynlais fell from £3426 in 1923 to £391 in 1929, at Glanyllyn from £17,820 to £479, and at Upper Boat from £1886 to £1054. Little wonder the line was singled in 1928 and closed in 1931.

However, the first casualty had been the Sunday service which the GW had maintained at four each way from 1922 to 1926. An Emergency Timetable, issued when the General Strike had finished but with the Miners' strike still on, allowed a modified service to operate, but dropped the Sunday service entirely. That timetable was dated 6th June, 1926, and the Sunday service did not re-appear in the normal

CARDIFF and RHYDYFELIN (Motor Cars—1st and 3rd class).—Cardiff.

Gen. Man., C. S. Denniss. Chief Eng., H. S. C. Ree. Traffic Supt., W. J. Holloway. Sec., H. A. Roberts.

Up.		Week Days.													Sundays.				
Rhymney Station,	mrn	mrn	mrn	mrn	mrn	aft	aft	aft	aft	aft	aft	aft		aft		aft	aft	aft	aft	aft
Cardiff ¶ ....dep.	5 10	7 15	8 38	9 55	1122	1	5 2	30	3 55	5 18	6 50	8 40	10 5	1120		1245	2 30	4 10	6 19	8 30
Whitchurch ¶	5 18	7 28	8 51	10 8	1135	18	2 43	4	8 5	3 17	3 8	53	1018	1133		1258	2 43	4 23	6 32	8 43
Tongwynlais ¶	5 22	7 34	8 57	1016	1141	1 24	2 49	4 14	5 37	7 9	8 59	1024		1139		1 4	2 49	4 29	6 38	8 49
Glanyllyn ¶	5 27	7 39	9 2	1021	1146	1 29	2 54	4 19	5 42	7 14	9 4	1029		1144		1 9	2 54	4 34	6 43	8 54
Upper Boat	5 32	7 46	9 7	1026	1153	1 36	3 0	4 26	5 49	7 21	9 11	1036		1150		1 15	3 0	4 40	6 49	9 0
Rhydyfelin Halt ...arr.	5 34	7 49	9 10	1029	1156	1 39	3 4	4 29	5 52	7 24	9 14	1039		1153		1 18	3 4	4 36	5 29	9 3

Down.		Week Days.													Sundays.				
	mrn	mrn	mrn	mrn	mrn	aft	aft	aft	aft	aft	aft	aft		aft		aft	aft	aft	aft	aft
Rhydyfelin Halt ...dep.	5 39		8 1	9 20	1044	1226	1 52	3 17	4 40	6 12	8 1	9 26	1045	12 0		1 53	3 35	4 27	5 3	9 13
Upper Boat ¶	5 42		8 4	9 23	1047	1230	1 55	3 20	4 43	6 15	8 4	9 29	1048	12 3		1 56	3 36	5 45	7 56	9 16
Glanyllyn ¶	5 47		8 10	9 29	1053	1236	2 1	3 26	4 49	6 21	8 10	9 35	1053	12 8		2 2	2 3	4.25	5 18	9 22
Tongwynlais ¶	5 52		8 16	9 34	1058	1241	2 6	3 31	4 54	6 26	8 15	9 40	1058	1218		2 7	3 47	5 56	8 7	9 27
Whitchurch ¶	5 57	6 55	8 21	9 39	11 4	1247	2 12	3 37	5 0	6 32	8 21	9 46	11 4	12 9		2 13	2 53	6 2	8 13	9 33
Cardiff (Rhymney)..arr.		7 10	8 34	9 51	1118	1	1 2	25	3 51	5 14	6 46	8 35	10 0	1115		1230	2 26	6 6	15 8	26	9 46

¶ "Halts" at Heath and Rhubina, between Cardiff and Whitchurch; Coryton, between Whitchurch and
Tongwynlais; and Nantgarw, between Glanyllyn and Upper Boat.

October 1911 Timetable

CARDIFF AND RHYDYFELIN
(CARDIFF RAILWAY).

		Week Days.												Sundays.			
	W	W				W					W						
	a.m.	a.m.	a.m.	a.m.	p.m.	p.m.	p.m.	p.m.	p.m.		p.m.	p.m.		p.m.	p.m.		p.m.	p.m.
Cardiff (R.R.) ¶ ...dep.	5 20	7 0	8 30	9 52	1 5	2 30	3 55	5 22	6 45	...	8 3	9 30		2 40	4 5	...	6 10	8 30
Heath "	5 27	7 7	8 37	9 59	112	2 37	4 2	5 29	6 52	...	8 10	9 37		2 47	4 12	...	6 17	8 37
Rhiwbina "	5 31	7 11	8 41	10 3	116	2 41	4 6	5 33	6 56	...	8 14	9 41		2 51	4 16	...	6 21	8 41
Whitchurch "	5 33	7 13	8 43	10 6	118	2 43	4 8	5 35	6 59	...	8 16	9 43		2 53	4 18	...	6 23	8 43
Coryton "	5 25	7 15	8 45	10 8	120	2 45	4 10	5 37	7 0	...	8 18	9 45		2 55	4 20	...	6 25	8 45
Tongwynlais "	5 30	7 19	8 49	10 12	124	2 49	4 14	5 41	7 4	...	8 22	9 49		2 59	424	...	6 29	8 49
Glanyllyn "	5 44	7 24	8 54	10 17	1 29	2 54	4 19	5 46	7 9	...	8 27	9 54		3 4	129	...	6 34	8 54
Nantgarw "	5 46	7 26	8 56	10 19	1 31	2 56	4 21	5 48	7 11	...	8 29	9 56		3 6	4 31	...	6 36	8 56
Upper Boat "	5 51	7 31	9 1	10 24	1 36	3 1	4 25	5 53	7 16	...	8 34	10 0		3 10	4 35	...	6 40	9 0
Rhydyfelin Halt ...arr.	5 53	7 34	9 4	10 27	1 39	3 4	4 28	5 56	7 19	...	8 37	10 3		3 13	4 38	...	6 44	9 3

	a.m.	a.m.	a.m.	p.m.	W	W	W		W									
					p.m.	p.m.	p.m.	p.m.	p.m.		p.m.	p.m.		p.m.	p.m.		p.m.	p.m.
Rhydyfelin Halt ......dep.	6 10	7 50	9 14	1225	152	3 17	4 42	6 7	7 25	...	8 50	1020		3 25	5 30	...	7 53	9 13
Upper Boat "	6 13	7 53	9 17	1228	1 55	3 20	4 45	6 10	7 28	...	8 53	1023		3 28	5 33	...	7 56	9 16
Nantgarw "	6 17	7 57	9 21	1232	169	3 24	4 49	6 14	7 32	...	8 57	1026		3 31	5 37	...	8 0	9 20
Glanyllyn "	6 20	8 0	9 23	1235	2 1	3 26	4 52	6 16	7 34	...	8 59	1029		3 34	5 39	...	8 2	9 22
Tongwynlais "	6 25	8 5	9 28	1240	2 6	3 31	4 57	6 21	7 39	...	9 4	1034		3 39	5 44	...	8 7	9 27
Coryton "	6 29	8 9	9 32	1244	2 10	3 35	5 1	6 25	7 43	...	9 8	1038		3 43	5 48	...	8 11	9 31
Whitchurch "	6 31	8 11	9 33	1246	2 12	3 37	5 3	6 27	7 45	...	9 10	1040		3 45	5 50	...	8 13	9 33
Rhiwbina "	6 33	8 13	9 35	1248	2 14	3 39	5 5	6 29	7 47	...	9 12	1042		3 47	5 52	...	8 15	9 35
Heath "	6 38	8 18	9 40	1253	2 18	3 44	5 10	6 34	7 52	...	9 17	1047		3 53	5 56	...	3 19	9 39
Cardiff (R.R.) ¶ ...arr.	6 44	8 25	9 47	1 0	2 25	3 50	5 17	6 40	7 58	...	9 24	1054		4 0	6 4	...	8 26	9 46

W—Workmen's Tickets are only available by these trains. ¶—About 1 mile from G.W. Station.

The Train Service between Cardiff (R.R.) and Rhydyfelin is subject to alteration. Passengers should consult the Cardiff Railway Company's announcements.

1921 Passenger Timetable

Former RR 0–6–2T No. 37 with a train of coke from Nantgarw approaching Tongwynlais tunnel, 12th May, 1952.   *R.C. Riley*

2–6–2T No. 4589 propels an auto train ex Coryton from Cardiff Queen Street Station for Bute Road, 6th October, 1953. (The trailer cars are ex-TVR, of 1907/12 vintage.)   *S. Rickard*

Former RR 0–6–2T No. 42 about to leave Nantgarw with a loaded coal train in August 1957. (The last turn of duty for No. 42 before withdrawal was on 24th August, 1957.) *Derek Chaplin*

The fireman of 2–6–2T No. 5572 takes the Staff for the single line section to Coryton, at Whitchurch, October 1957. *Derek Chaplin*

An SLS railtour stands on the CR section at Nantgarw, 12th July, 1958; 0–6–0PT No. 6434 heads trailers 177 and 225. *Author*

Early morning at Whitchurch Station. The first DMU of the day on the Coryton branch stands at the up platform, whilst an 84XX 0–6–0PT shunts the daily goods; 23rd August, 1961. *John White*

timetable issued on 12th July, hence the last Sunday trains to actually run were on 2nd May, 1926, the strike starting the following day.

At the southern end of the line the weekday service to Whitchurch had increased to seven each way by July 1927 and to eleven each way twelve months later, when the line was singled beyond Whitchurch. The singling of the line north of Whitchurch presented little problem to this north Cardiff suburban service, several of the halt platforms were lengthened as previously recorded, and a new halt opened at Birchgrove, between Heath and Rhiwbina Halts, on 10th June, 1929. Thus when the split came as from 20th July, 1931, there was virtually no traffic, passenger, parcel, goods or mineral, on the northern section of the line, but a flourishing suburban passenger service into Cardiff. However, when planning the split, it was realized that there was increasing passenger traffic at Coryton, and that it was well within the Cardiff commuter belt hence, despite the line having been singled beyond Whitchurch, Coryton Halt became the terminus of the new service. This must have been a late decision as, besides the singling which would involve staff working, there were no platforms at Coryton, as it had been expected to close with the remainder of the single line section, neither was there a run around loop.

Despite these problems the new north Cardiff suburban service commenced with no less than 22 trains each way weekdays and 21 on Saturdays. These had to be auto trains of course, without any turn around facilities at Coryton but, as already stated in Part Two, a new halt, two chains nearer Cardiff, and with a raised platform on the up side, was quickly provided and a run around loop put in the following year. However, the short section of single line between Whitchurch North and Coryton always meant it had to be controlled by the single line and tablet instructions. The auto services were still mainly in the hands of rebuilt ex-TVR 'M1' class 0–6–2Ts which were fast and clean starters from the many halts, but GWR 0–6–0 auto fitted pannier tanks also did a fair share of this work; the one most remembered was No. 2066 which was employed from late 1935 onwards.

By that time the new '4800' class auto fitted 0–4–2Ts had performed on the branch, but these never established themselves as the '6400' class auto fitted 0–6–0PTs did, and the latter were regulars on the branch until three car diesel suburban sets took over, in stages, from June 1958 onwards. The five coach trains which were used on the branch at peak periods, were initially mainly hauled by ex-Taff Vale 'A' class 0–6–2Ts, sometimes by the GWR 0–6–2Ts of the '5600' class, and occasionally by ex-Rhymney Railway 0–6–2Ts. By the mid 1950s, 2–6–2Ts of the '4100' class were regular performers, whilst from September 1953 onwards the small 2–6–2Ts of the '4575' class did a fair amount of auto work on the branch, but never fully ousted the '6400' pannier tanks, which were a very popular auto-fitted class with the footplate crews in east South Wales.

During both World Wars ambulance trains were run through to Whitchurch, for the nearby military hospital. During World War I the Cardiff Railway service was suspended when an ambulance train was expected. Although full details of the motive power used have not been traced it is known that such trains were worked to Whitchurch by GWR engines, usually double headed by a pair of 0–6–0STs. During World War II the usual motive power was a pair of '5600' class 0–6–2Ts, although it has been said that a pair of ex-Great Eastern inside cylinders 4–6–0s once worked to Whitchurch. This is distinctly possible, as some of those engines worked in pairs on ambulance trains throughout Southern England and Wales, and the author personally remembers one such pair heading an ambulance train down the old Monmouthshire Railway line, between Cwmbran and Newport Dock Street, one sunny Summer evening during the later stages of the war.

However, back to the passenger service on the branch itself. A very high level of service was provided until the second War, when the service was curtailed to 17 each way by the War Emergency timetable issued on 25th September, 1939. This was restored to 24 each way (22 on Saturdays) in 1940, but was cut again to 21 (20 Saturdays) in 1942, a service that remained fairly constant for the next few years. The service was increased by one train daily in 1945, but cut to 19 trains, with one extra on Saturdays, in the early 1950s.

When a regular interval service was introduced to the main routes in the Cardiff Valleys (but not to the Coryton branch) on 21st September, 1953, the service was improved to 24 trains (23 Saturdays), although one train was taken off the following year. In 1959 there was a cut-back to 20 trains daily, but this still reasonable service took a severe knock in 1962 when it was reduced to 14 trains, and run only at peak periods for commuter traffic. As already recorded, BR tried to close the branch the following year under the Beeching economies, but this was prevented by the opposition of the well heeled residents of north Cardiff, although BR responded by further cutting the service to 11 trains each way, which had been further cut to 10 by 1972.

For many years the service has only provided for the morning rush hour traffic, a brief mid-day service, and again at close of work, with no evening, or Saturday afternoon service at all. In the past year or two there has been a distinct change of heart by BR with regard to Cardiff Valleys passenger services, resulting in some new stations

A football excursion from Coryton to Ninian Park platform leaves Whitchurch headed by 0–6–2T No. 5648 on Saturday 14th October, 1961.   *John White*

2–6–2T No. 4177 (known locally as "The Pride of the Valleys") heads a return football excursion at Birchgrove Halt, 20th October, 1962.   *John White*

The first "Sprinter" DMU on the Coryton branch, negotiates the short spur from the new Heath Jn to Heath (LL), 2nd February, 1985.   *John White*

Three car DMU at Coryton terminus, 17th April, 1986.   *Bob Pugh*

and others planned, and also the proposed north to west Inner Cardiff "circular" service which has been described in Part Two. When this comes to pass it will revolutionise the Coryton branch service, with the probability of a half hourly service. Already (in 1985) the service has been increased to 15 trains daily, although one is unusual – the 18.02 from Coryton – in that it runs non-stop from Coryton to Cardiff Queen Street. The others stop at all halts (now classed as stations of course) *en route* in both directions. The new timetable includes a regular hourly service at off peak periods during the day, i.e. from around 10.00 hrs to around 16.00 hrs. It also provides a Saturday service of 12 trains each way, again based on an hourly interval service, commencing at 07.40 and finishing at 19.16. Sunday services were never resumed after the sudden closure in 1926 but, at the time of writing these notes, the future for the branch looks far more hopeful than it has looked in the past 23 years.

Mineral and Goods services

On the freight side there is little to record. In Cardiff Railway days two such trains were booked through to Rhydyfelin (although it is unlikely that they often went beyond Upper Boat station). These trains called at the four stations, the private sidings at Birchgrove and Portobello, and at Nantgarw as required. It seems probable that on frequent occasions the second goods train of the day was not required. In the final couple of years before the amalgamation a separate mineral train, to serve the colliery, was added to the timetable. These trains were normally hauled by the robust 0–6–2Ts Nos. 33 to 35, built in 1908, although older 0–6–2Ts would be used when the '33' class was not available.

When the GWR took over in 1922, two night mineral trains were booked to Nantgarw Colliery, from which good tonnages were then expected. There was also one ordinary goods train to Upper Boat and back, serving the stations and sidings as in pre-group days. From 1st January, 1926, one mineral and one goods train sufficed, although an extra local goods was put on from Cardiff serving the Brick Works at Birchgrove and Whitchurch goods shed only. By 1930 one goods train per week to Upper Boat was sufficient, plus the daily service to Whitchurch. Although there is no record available of the motive power during that period, it is thought that the ex-Cardiff Railway 0–6–2Ts handled most of the traffic, with ex-Rhymney 0–6–2Ts or GWR 0–6–0PTs filling in as necessary, the latter particularly on the Whitchurch turn.

After the closure of the northern section the Whitchurch goods continued to run, normally one early morning train was sufficient, but this was increased to two daily during the War years, when extra sidings were put in at Birchgrove for military traffic. After the war the service reverted to one train daily, and continued to run until Whitchurch goods closed as from 2nd December, 1963. The motive power in later days was usually a GW (or WR) pannier tank, at first of the '5700'/'8750' class, but later often one of the tapered boiler '8400' class.

Since that date the branch has had a passenger service only, using three car diesel suburban sets, and the only other power to use the branch has been the occasional class 37 diesel with the District Engineer's saloon, or one of the same class on PW trains, and also various items of Engineering Dept On-Track plant, such as tampers, track liners etc.

At the northern end of the line the survivor of the Cardiff Railway '33' class 0–6–2Ts, GW No. 155, was a regular on the freight trains that passed over the re-opened northern section north of Coryton, from 1948 onwards. Rhymney 'A1' class 0–6–2Ts were also employed when No. 155 was not available. When coal started to flow down the line the usual motive power was one of the former Rhymney 'AR' class 0–6–2Ts, most of which were still carrying Rhymney pattern boilers. These were finally withdrawn from service late in 1957, well after the new link to the former Taff Vale section at Taffs Well had been opened, over which the Rhymney 'ARs' continued to handle nearly all the traffic. For the brief period before class 37 diesels took over the working, pannier tanks of the '8400' class were used also '5600' class 0–6–2Ts. The Nantgarw Colliery branch is still powered by the class 37s, and there seems no reason why this is likely to change, the class being ideally suited to South Wales coal traffic.

Signalling

The Cardiff Railway and its predecessors at the docks, employed McKenzie Holland and Co. of Worcester as their signal engineers. In this choice they were following their friends the Rhymney Railway, and several other railways in South Wales who also used McKenzie Holland, their distinctive somersault signals, with their tall spiked mushroom type finials, being a feature of the local railways for the best part of 80 years, the last examples not being taken down until the 1960s.

The Cardiff Railway Appendix of 1909 lists no less than 25 signal cabins owned or jointly owned within the docks area and doubtless, there were a few others owned and operated by the other railways that worked within the docks confines. Four of the cabins were

Tyndall Street Crossing signal box, *c.*1906.   *F. Equeall*

North East Jn signal box, a GWR replacement for the original CR box; photographed 5th April, 1978.   *Keith Jones*

glorified ground frames, two were operated by the men in charge of swing bridges, one similarly for controlling a caisson, but the fourth carried the delightful Victorian name *Tyndall Street Cart Road Crossing*.

The other 21 were all standard type cabins, known as "Elevated Cabins" in the CR Appendix. These McKenzie boxes were either constructed of grey stone for the lower half housing the bottom of the levers and linkage, with a timber top section for the signalman and his levers or, with some of the later boxes, entirely of timber on a grey stone dwarf base. *Roath Basin Junction* cabin was jointly owned by the Great Western, Rhymney and Cardiff Railways, whilst two others were listed as jointly owned by two of the companies. Several had names that gave the atmosphere of dock working ie *Maloney's Tip Junction, Quadruple Crossing Cabin, West Side Roath Basin Swing Bridge, Fuel Works Branch Junction* and so on. The full list was:

No.	Name	Type	Notes
1.	West Dock Swing Bridge	Ground Cabin	Signals interlocked with catch points and bridge.
2.	Junction Dry Dock Caisson	" "	Signals interlocked with catch points & Caisson.
3.	Maloneys Tip Junction	Elevated Cabin	
4.	East Dock Jn (High Level)	" "	
5.	Tyndall Street Junction	" "	RR & CR Joint
6.	Junction Canal Swing Bridge	Ground Cabin	Signals interlocked with catch points and bridge.
7.	Tyndall St Cart Road Crossing	" "	
8.	East Moors Junction	Elevated Cabin	
9.	Tyndall Street Crossing	" "	GWR & CR Joint
10.	Roath Basin Junction	" "	GWR, RR & CR Joint
11.	East Dock Crossing	" "	
12.	Quadruple Crossing Cabin	" "	
13.	West Side Roath Basin Swing Bridge	" "	
14.	Rhymney Crossing Cabin	" "	
15.	Stonefield Junction	" "	
16.	Roath Dock Swing Bridge	" "	
17.	Fuel Works Branch Junction	" "	
18.	Roath Dock Junction	" "	
19.	North East Junction	" "	
20.	Splott Junction	" "	
21.	South East Cabin	" "	
22.	Roath Dock South Cabin	" "	
23.	King's Junction	" "	
24.	East Cabin	" "	
25.	West Cabin	" "	

PHŒNIX BRICK WORKS AND GROVE WIRE ROPE COMPANIES' SIDINGS.

These Sidings are between Heath Junction and Whitchurch, and have a connection with the Up Line only. Both lots of Sidings are served by the same connection, which is worked from a Ground Frame by the Guards. Traffic for the direction of Heath Junction is taken to Whitchurch Station and brought back from there.

WORKING AT CORYTON HALT.

When it is necessary for an Engine to run round coaches at Coryton Halt, the Driver must not, when proceeding through the Loop, take the Engine beyond a point opposite the Whitchurch end of the Halt Platform, unless and until such time as he has received a hand signal from the Guard, as an intimation that the Catch Point at the Whitchurch end of the Loop has been properly closed, and the Loop points set for the engine to pass out of the Loop on to the Single Line.

WORKING BEYOND CORYTON HALT IN THE DIRECTION OF RHYDYFELIN.

Whenever it is necessary for a Train to go beyond Coryton Halt, the Driver must be handed the Staff Whitchurch-Coryton and the Guard must obtain from the Signalman the key of the padlocks securing points between Coryton and Rhydyfelin. The Train must be accompanied by a second Traffic man Whitchurch to Coryton. After the Train has gone clear of the Catch Point on the Single Line at Coryton, three detonators must be placed on the Line one hundred yards on the Rhydyfelin side of the Catch Point, and the second Traffic man must immediately return to Whitchurch with the Wooden Train Staff, and hand it back to the Signalman, who must make an entry in the Train Register accordingly. The second Traffic man must then return to the detonators and remain there until the train arrives back, when he must go to Whitchurch and the Signalman there must hand the Wooden Train Staff Whitchurch-Coryton to him as soon as he can do so without delaying the Passenger Train service, and a note must be made in the Train Register.

The second Traffic man must convey the Wooden Staff to the Guard of the Train, who must unlock the Ground Frame on the Rhydyfelin side of Coryton Platform, close the Catch Point on the Single Line, pull off the disc and set the spring points leading to the Loop for the Platform Line over which Line the Train must run. After the Train has passed clear, all points and disc must be restored to normal and the Staff handed to the Driver, who will give it up at Whitchurch in the usual manner. The Guard must also return the Padlock Key to the Whitchurch Signalman.

Trains must not be allowed to run on to the Single Line Coryton-Rhydyfelin during the hours of darkness.

Extract from the GWR Appendix to No. 9 section of the Service Timetable of 1st July, 1934.

CARDIFF RAILWAY COMPANY.

Rhyd-y-felin Terminal Halt.

A ground cabin named as above is fixed on the Down line side at the end of the crossover road for working the same and the following signals :—

Up Home signal fixed on the Up line side clear of the fouling point of the crossover road.

Down starting signal fixed on the Up line side at the southern end of the Halt Platform.

WHISTLES.

Up and Down Main lines	1 Long
Crossover road	1 Crow.

Nantgarw Colliery.

A ground frame named as above is fixed on the Down line side opposite the Down siding for working the same and the following signals :—

Down distant signal fixed on the Up line side 749 yards from Down home signal.

Down home signal fixed on the Down line side clear of the fouling point of the siding with the Down line.

WHISTLES.

Main Line	1 Long.
Down siding and Main line	1 Long and 1 Crow.

Extract from the Appendix to the General Rules and Regulations c.1911.

A Cardiff Railway docks map dated February 1917 shows amendments and additions to the above list, and also records which company operated jointly owned signal cabins:

Boxes 1 and 2 are not shown on the 1917 map, although this may only have indicated that they were not classed as signal boxes by that date.

Box 3 is shown as CR&TVR Joint, operated by Cardiff Railway.

Box 4 is shown as owned and operated by the TVR.

Box 5 is shown joint as 1909, operated by the Rhymney Railway.

Box 9 is shown joint as 1909, operated by Cardiff Railway.

Box 10 is shown joint as 1909, operated by the GWR.

Boxes 11 and 12 are shown as jointly owned by the GWR, RR and CR, and operated by GWR.

Box 20 is shown as jointly owned by the CR&GWR, and operated by the CR.

Box 24 is given as Queen Alexandra Dock Entrance East.

Box 25 is given as Queen Alexandra Dock Entrance West.

The following additional cabins are shown:

Roath Branch South (not in use)	Owned jointly by CR and GWR.
Roath Dock Storage	Owned and operated by TVR.
LNWR Cabin	Located east of East Dock, worked by RR.
LNWR Cabin (Cardiff Yard)	Located Tyndall Street Yard, owned and operated by LNWR.

Many of the cabins were renewed during the period of GWR ownership of the docks, and sometimes two were combined to form one new box, *Tyndall Street Junction* box was still in use until the former Rhymney Railway connection to the docks was taken out late in 1964. *South East Junction* lasted until the late 1970s although that was a box of modern BR design which replaced the original box which burned down in the 1960s. *North East Junction* lasted until 1979, although that box (the shell of which was still *in situ* 1/1986) was a 1935 GWR replacement for the original McKenzie Holland.

When construction of the Cardiff Railway main line was completed early in 1909, McKenzie Holland again erected the signal cabins and supplied the equipment. In fact there was so much McKenzie Holland signalling in east South Wales that the firm maintained a local yard and office, to be readily available to maintain the equipment they had supplied. As far as can be ascertained the new cabins were constructed entirely of timber upon dwarf walls. At the junction with the Rhymney Railway a further cabin, Heath South, was put in for the opening of the new railway in 1911. This was a Rhymney Railway box although, doubtless, the cost was borne by the Cardiff

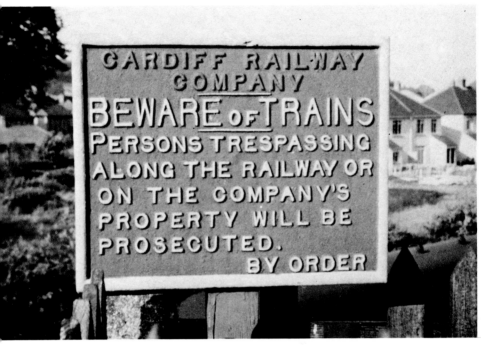

Cardiff Railway trespass notice at Rhiwbina Halt, still in use in the mid 1950s.
Alan Jarvis

Ground frame name plate.   *Ian Wright*

Railway The full list of new boxes etc., put in for the new line was:

Name	Type of Box	No. of Levers Working	Spare	Location
Heath South	Elevated Cabin	(RR Cabin)		On down side of RR at Jn.
Heath Sidings West	„ „	13	2	On downside 22c west of Jn.
Whitchurch Station	„ „	17	3	At Cardiff end of down platform.
Tongwynlais Station	„ „	17	4	„ „ „ „
Portobello Quarry Siding	„ „	9	3	On upside opposite Quarry Siding.
Glan-y-Llyn Station	„ „	19	6	At back of down platform.
Nantgarw Colliery	Ground Frame	3	Nil	On downside opp. down siding.
Upper Boat Station	Elevated Cabin	16	6	At north end of down platform.
Rhyd-y-Felin Terminal Halt	Ground Cabin	3	1	On downside end of crossover.

Without the expected Taff Vale Railway supporting trains, it quickly became apparent that the meagre traffic on the Cardiff line did not warrant the luxury of so many signal boxes, hence one of the economy measures quickly introduced was that all cabins north of Heath Sidings West should be classed as "Opened only as required for traffic purposes" thus becoming, more or less, covered ground frames, and that remained the pattern for the rest of the company's independent existence.

However, at Nantgarw Colliery the position was somewhat reversed. Anticipating far more traffic then actually resulted from the developed colliery, a new signal box replaced the ground frame in 1921, although that was also "Opened as required" as with the other cabins.

The position altered little in very early GWR days, although the increased traffic in the north Cardiff area resulted in Whitchurch box being manned in 1925, in addition to Heath West. By September 1927 the boxes north of Whitchurch were omitted altogether from the list in the working time tables, these were replaced by ground frames as the line was singled, completed in May 1928. Passing loops were retained at Tongwynlais, Nantgarw Colliery, and Upper Boat, in each case two ground frames were provided, one north and one south of the station/colliery. The run around loop at Rhydyfelin, with its existing ground frame, was also retained. Another ground frame was put in at the north side of Glan-y-Llyn Station, to cover a siding left in.

At the junction with the RR section, the GWR put in a new Heath Junction box sited in the triangle between the two sets of lines. This opened late in 1927, and dispensed with the former RR boxes Heath South and Heath North, and the former CR box Heath West (formerly Heath Sidings West).

After the loop was put in at Coryton Halt in 1932, ground frames were put in at both the north and south ends of the loop, although it is possible that a ground frame had existed at the north end since July 1931, when the line north of that point was closed to all traffic, but remained *in situ* pending possible developments at Nantgarw Colliery. As the "closed" line was often used for wagon storage, catch points had been put in to protect the running line from Coryton southwards, hence a ground frame was probably put in at that time, and modified to cover the loop the following year.

A further box opened at Birchgrove in 1942 to cover the new sidings mentioned in the Railway Section, whilst a small box was put in at the southern end of Nantgarw Colliery sidings when the colliery was developed by the NCB in 1952. Birchgrove and Whitchurch boxes were both closed as from 14th June, 1964, leaving Heath Junction box to entirely control the (by then) Coryton branch, on the "one engine in steam" principle. Nantgarw box was closed later in 1964 when block working on the Nantgarw Colliery branch was abolished.

The remaining box at Heath Junction stayed in use until the new junction opened on 19th November, 1984, when it was replaced by a new ground level cabin which controls the branch electronically through track circuiting at the junction. This will not permit a train to enter the branch until the previous train on the branch has been entirely cleared by the return circuit.

DIRECTORS, MANAGEMENT, HEAD OFFICE

From the opening of the West Dock in 1839, at least until February 1845, the second Marquis of Bute, with the assistance of his advisers, took all the major decisions re the working of the dock, but at that date he set up a Trusteeship of three, to look after the dock and his estates in the Cardiff area on his behalf, although there was a proviso that he could veto, during his lifetime, any of their decisions. After his death in 1848, the authority of the Trustees was established by the Marquis's Will, and as the third Marquis was an infant born the

The elaborate relief on the west wall of the Pierhead Building, 28th
November, 1985. *Welsh Industrial and Maritime Museum, Cardiff*

The circular mosaic in the flooring at the main entrance to the Pierhead
Building.   *Welsh Industrial and Maritime Museum, Cardiff*

Presentation at the retirement of the Whitchurch station master, Tom
Marsden, *c.*1930. The group comprises officials and staff of the former CR,
and includes the Tongwynlais station master (*centre*) and guard Tom Meyrick
(*right*).   *John White Collection*

previous year, the Trustees were entirely responsible for looking after his interests.

It was in April 1852 that John Boyle became one of the Trustees, and within some three years he became the Managing Trustee, and made all the major decisions for many years. As Chairman of the Rhymney Railway as well, it was his decision to give trading preference to that railway at the new Bute East Dock in the later 1850s and 1860s, that led to the series of confrontations between the RR and TVR which continued for most of the remainder of the period of Trusteeship.

The Bute Docks Company was created with effect from 1st January, 1887, after which a Board of Directors (which included some of the former Trustees) replaced the Trustees, with a Managing Director responsible for any major day-to-day decisions that had to be taken. The change of name to the Cardiff Railway in 1897 did not affect that policy initially, and Lord Merthyr, with long experience of the coal trade in South Wales, was the Managing Director for many years. However, in view of his Lordship's ill health in 1909/10, and with their new railway into the Taff Valley virtually completed, the Directors decided to appoint a General Manager to lead the existing officials, both those covering the docks and the new railway.

The man chosen, early in 1910, was Lieut Col Charles S. Denniss who had been GM and Secretary of the Cambrian Railways since 1895, and who had had previous experience with both the North Eastern and Great Western Railways. He was at the helm in a difficult period, with on/off confrontations with the Taff Vale Railway, a main line of his own that was virtually doomed before it started, and with one of the largest and busiest docks in the United Kingdom which was not giving the financial return to its investors that the massive volume of traffic warranted. Due to wartime conditions Col Denniss retired at the start of April 1917, to make way for closer working arrangements between the Cardiff, Taff Vale and Rhymney Railways. These three companies were unified under one common general manager, and Mr E.A. Prosser of the Rhymney was put in charge. That was the position when all three became constituent companies of the Great Western Railway as from 25th March, 1922 (backdated to take effect as from 1st January, 1922).

The South Wales docks were somewhat remote, and unfamiliar to be entirely controlled from Paddington, hence this became the responsibility of a chief docks manager, based at the former Cardiff Railway HQ at Pierhead Building, Cardiff Docks, with separate dock managers at each of the major South Wales ports for day to day decisions. Hence under the GWR Cardiff had both a chief docks

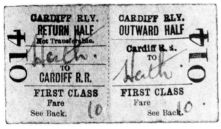

Selection of Cardiff Railway tickets.   *David Geldard*

Medallion struck to commemorate the opening of the Queen Alexandra
Dock, 13th July, 1907.
                                          Derek Robinson

manager and dock manager. The short section of Cardiff Railway main line was swallowed up into the newly created Cardiff Valleys Division of the GWR, which lasted until the Welsh Division of British Railways was set up, with HQ at Cardiff, in 1960.

Back at the docks, no major changes were made to the management structure for the remainder of the GWR's existence, and Cardiff – along with the other ports – passed into British Railways ownership as from 1st January, 1948. The Docks and Inland Waterways Executive was formed on 1st August, 1948 to control British Transport Docks, with little change of management structure as far as the South Wales ports were concerned, and the Pierhead Building as the local HQ. In 1963 the British Transport Docks Board was created, with the nationalised ports administered as a separate identity in their own right. By that time only five South Wales ports – Cardiff, Newport, Barry, Port Talbot and Swansea remained, each with individual dock managers responsible to the area HQ at Cardiff's Pierhead Building. However, it was during this régime that Cardiff and other South Wales docks were transported from decaying coal exporting docks, with miles of rusting sidings, to multi-purpose ports, with modern handling facilities connected to the major motorways, as well as to rail freightliner depots. The South Wales HQ was still at Cardiff.

That was the position until 31st December, 1982 when Associated British Ports took over the responsibility for the formerly publicly owned ports. The Pierhead Building remained as an administrative building, known as the South Wales Group Office, embracing the port manager's office (covering Barry Docks as well as Cardiff) along with an operations office.

The offices of the Bute Docks Co. were at the bottom end of Bute Street, Cardiff, on a site later occupied by the Powell Duffryn building, but that early office was destroyed by fire on 19th November, 1892. The staff were then moved to Victoria Building, also in Bute Street where they remained until the magnificent structure known as Pierhead Building opened in August 1897.

William Frame was the architect of this imposing and ornate building. He had been assistant to William Burges, architect to the third Marquis of Bute, whose outstanding work included the restoration in Gothic style of Cardiff Castle and the re-creation of Castell Coch as a medieval style fortress; this still stands high up on the eastern hillside of the lower Taff valley overlooking Tongwynlais. Frame was also assistant on that project until Burges' death, and then succeeded him.

The new offices, which stand at the southern end of the parcel of land which formerly separated the West and East Dock basins, face south-west, overlooking the entrance channel to the docks and the Bristol Channel. Built of the finest quality red brick with elaborate terracotta finishing, it has an imposing feudal style tower, with turret surrounds, one large panel on the west side depicting two shields, one with the arms of the old borough of Cardiff, the other with the arms of the Bute family. Over the shields stands a small tank locomotive whilst below is a sailing ship. Below the panel are the words WRTH DDWR A THAN, "By fire and water", denoting the change from a purely dock company, to a railway dock owning company, at the time the building was under erection. Once again the Gothic style of Burges/Frame is the main feature of the design of the building and its tower.

Below the tower is the main entrance hall, which has an ornate circular mosaic panel on the lines of the outside panel, with the arms depicting a locomotive and a sailing ship. (On this panel the locomotive is shown as a 4–4–0 tender engine, without tender, whilst the engine on the outside panel is a 2–4–0T. It is a matter of curiosity why these were chosen, as far as is known the Bute locomotive stock never included a 2–4–0T and certainly never a tender engine at all!) The dock manager's office has elaborated mediaeval style joinery, complemented with oriel windows, coffered ceiling and equally elaborate canopied fireplace. The main office block, on the ground floor, is also on an ornate scale, resembling a large church-like hall, divided by two arcades of large semi-circular arches. Altogether, a most impressive building.

The Coat of Arms of the Cardiff Railway was not so elaborate as its local neighbours, the Taff Vale and Barry railways, with the Taff's mountain goat and the Barry's Welsh dragon catching the eye and providing Welsh flavour. Nevertheless it was a quiet, pleasing crest, with the two shields and their arms tilting towards each other, with the same four Welsh words again appearing, two above and two below the shields, this central piece surrounded by a roped edged circular band on which the words CARDIFF RAILWAY COMPANY appear in plain, unshaded lettering.

The company staff uniform buttons continued the same combination of locomotive and sailing ship as the panels at the Pierhead building. On the top half circle of the button appeared a small locomotive (a 2–2–2 this time!), with a three masted sailing ship on the lower half, and the words CARDIFF RAILWAY around the two in semi-circular fashion.

Two other relevant uniform buttons are known to have been issued, but it is not certain whether these were Bute Docks Co. buttons or even Bute Trustees (or both), or simply worn by the Marine Department at the docks in Cardiff Railway days. One was of simple design, with a ships anchor in the centre surrounded by circular lettering, with the words BUTE DOCKS.

The other, more elaborate, had the same wording around the top half circle, but the centre had two motifs, the coronet of Lord Bute at the top, with an anchor in the lower half. This attractive button suggests the Bute Trustees period, as the coronet motif was also used to adorn the Marquis locomotive stock prior to the formation of the Docks Co. in 1887.

Passenger train tickets followed the standard pattern of the period. They were of the Edmunson's card type and, despite the meagre size of the railway, covered all the more usual types such as singles, returns, day returns, excursions, workmen's, child etc. Tickets to/from Cardiff were to CARDIFF RR of course, the Cardiff Railway having no station in the city centre. The word 'Halt' does not often appear on tickets the author has seen, merely Heath, Coryton, Nantgarw etc. without suffix.

Cardiff Railway "No Smoking" notice, 1920.
Welsh Industrial and Maritime Museum, Cardiff

Appendix A

Locomotive List Bute Trustees, Bute Dock Co., & Cardiff Railway

No.	Type		GW No.	Withdrawn or Renumbered
1		Not known		By 1882
1	0–6–0ST	Beyer Peacock 201/1860. Orig. No. 3, Renumbered 31 c.1894		(By 1894)
1	0–6–2T	Kitson 3580/1894	156	1931
2		Not known		By 1882
2	0–6–0PT	Kitson 2458/1882	693	1925
3	0–6–0ST	Beyer Peacock 201/1860. Ren'd 1 c.1882		(By 1882)
3	4–4–0T	Slaughter, Gruning & Co./1861 Ex North London Ry c.1882		By 1895
3	0–6–0T	Kitson 3602/1895	686	1925
4	0–6–0ST	Beyer Peacock 202/1860		By 1899
4	0–6–0T	Kitson 3871/1899	687	1925
5	0–4–0ST	Manning Wardle 46/1862		1898
5	0–4–0ST	Kitson 3799/1898	1338	1963
6	0–6–0ST	Manning Wardle 82/1863 (to Cardiff 1865)		c.1880
6	4–4–0T	Slaughter, Gruning & Co./1861 Ex North London Ry c.1882		c.1899
6	0–4–0ST	Kitson 3969/1899	1339	1932
7	0–6–0T	Manning Wardle 173/1866		1916
7	0–6–0T	Kitson 5182/1919	685	1931
8	0–6–0T	Manning Wardle 230/1868		1899
8	0–6–0T	Kitson 3872/1899	688	1926
9	0–6–0ST	Parfitt & Jenkins/1869		c.1898
9	0–6–2T	Kitson 3869/1898	157	1928
10	0–6–0ST	Parfitt & Jenkins/c.1870		c.1898
10	0–6–2T	Kitson 3870/1898	158	1932
11	0–6–0ST	Parfitt & Jenkins/1870–1		c.1898
11	0–6–2T	Kitson 4333/1905	160	1930
12	0–6–0ST	Parfitt & Jenkins/1871	694	1926
13		Not known		By 1882
13	4–4–0T	Slaughter Gruning & Co./1861 Ex North London Ry 1882		c.1895
13	0–6–0T	Kitson 3603/1895	690	1926
14	0–6–0ST	Parfitt & Jenkins/1872		1916
14	0–6–0ST	Hudswell Clarke 1404/1920	681	1955
15	0–6–0ST	Parfitt & Jenkins/1873	695	1926
16	0–6–0ST	Parfitt & Jenkins/1873		1919
16	0–6–0ST	Hudswell Clarke 1405/1920	682	1953
17	0–4–0ST	Fox Walker 200/1874		1916
17	0–6–0ST	Hudswell Clarke 1407/1920	683	1954
18	0–6–0ST	Parfitt & Jenkins/1875	696	1923

19	0–6–0ST	Parfitt & Jenkins/1875	697	1925
20	0–6–0ST	Parfitt & Jenkins/c.1877		1916
20	0–6–2T	Kitson 5180/1919	151	1930
21	0–6–0ST	Parfitt & Jenkins/c.1879		c.1905
21	0–6–2T	Kitson 4334/1905	161	1929
22	0–6–0ST	Parfitt & Jenkins/1880		1916
22	0–6–2T	Kitson 5181/1919	152	1936
23	0–6–0ST	Parfitt & Jenkins/1881		c.1906
23	0–6–0ST	GWR Swindon 1068/1886	1676	1926
		(to Cardiff 1907)		
24	0–6–0ST	Beyer Peacock/c.1860	(698)	1922
		(to Cardiff 1883)		
25	0–6–0ST	French Orig. Ex East and West Jn Ry		(1907)
		(to Cardiff 1885) Ren'd 32 – 1907		
25	0–6–0ST	GWR Swindon 1082/1887	1689	1931
		(to Cardiff 1907)		
26	0–6–2T	Kitson 2879/1886	163	1932
27	0–6–2T	Kitson 3068/1887	162	1932
28	0–6–2T	Kitson 3069/1887	159	1931
29	0–6–0T	Kitson 3132/1889	692	1929
30	0–6–0T	Kitson 3133/1889	691	1929
31	0–6–0ST	Beyer Peacock 201/1860 Ex No. 1 – 1894		1898
31	0–6–0ST	GWR Swindon 1059/1886	1667	1931
		(to Cardiff 1907)		
32	0–6–0ST	French Origin. Ex No. 25 – 1907		1916
32	0–6–0ST	Hudswell Clarke 1408/1920	684	1954
33	0–6–2T	Kitson 4595/1908	153	1930
34	0–6–2T	Kitson 4596/1908	154	1934
35	0–6–2T	Kitson 4597/1908	155	1953
36	2–4–2T	LNWR Crewe 3869/1879	(1327)	1922
		(to Cardiff 1914)		

Notes Nos. 23, 25 and 31 sold by GWR 12/1906 but not added to CR stock until 1907. Nos. 24 and 36 scrapped at Swindon May 1922 before GW numbers were actually allotted.

C. R.

(103)

TO

Rhydyfelin.

Selection of Locomotive Drawings of The Cardiff Railway

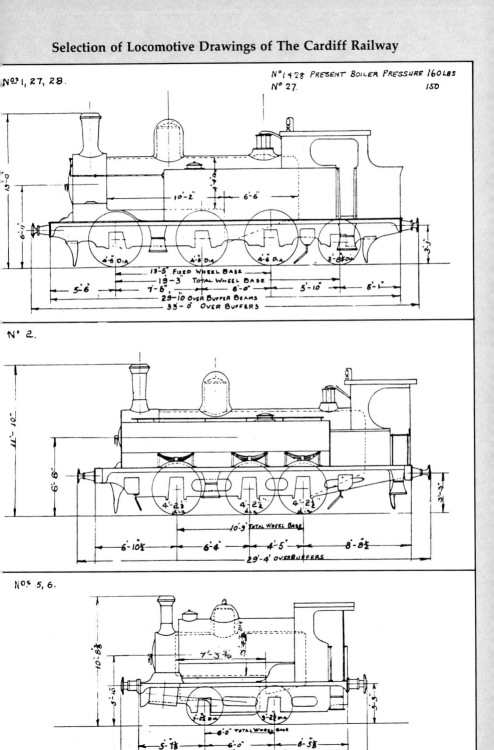

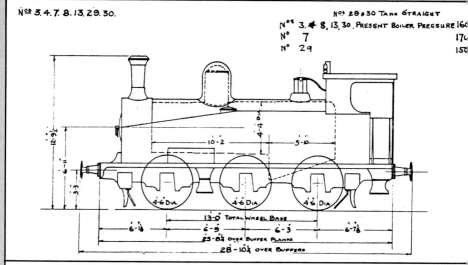

Nᵒˢ 3. 4. 7. 8. 13. 29. 30.

Nᵒˢ 28 & 30 TANK STRAIGHT
Nᵒˢ 3. 4 8. 13. 30. PRESENT BOILER PRESSURE 160
Nᵒ 7   170
Nᵒ 29   150

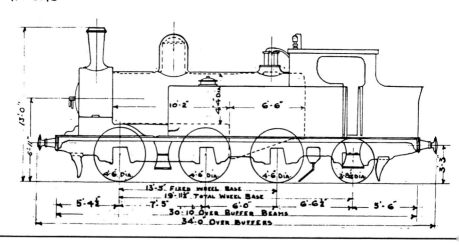

Nᵒˢ 9. 10

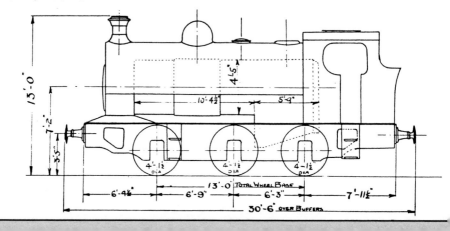

Nᵒˢ 14. 16 17. 32.

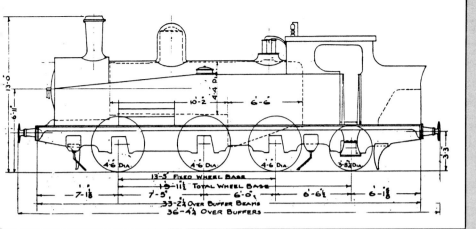

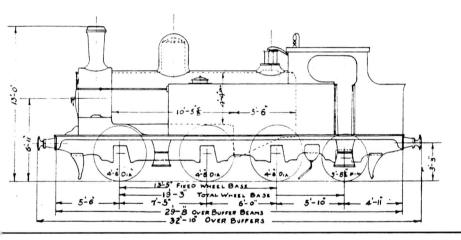

PRESENT BOILER PRESSURE REDUCED
TO 160 LBS.

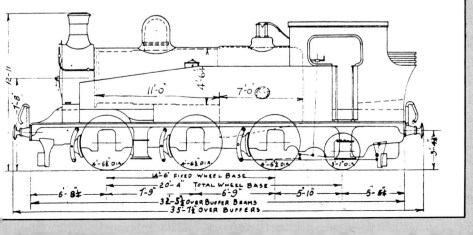

Summary of Bute Docks, Cardiff 1918

(also detailing the Tidal Harbour)

Name	Acts of Authorisation	Date opened	Deep Water Acres	Coaling Appliances	Closed to Shipping
West Dock	16.7.1830 22.5.1834	9.10.1839	19.5	12 Fixed	31.1.1964
East Dock	Constructed Privately	20.7.1855			
	Sanctioned by Act 5.7.1865	Extended 19.1.1858	46.25	17 Fixed	31.1.1970
		Extended 14.9.1859			
Tidal Harbour	Constructed Privately	13.8.1856		7 Fixed (1860)	July 1868
	Sanctioned by Act 5.7.1865				
Roath Basin	30.7.1866	23.7.1874	12	5 Fixed 4 Movable 1 Coaling Crane	Open
Roath Dock	16.7.1874 18.8.1882	24.8.1887	33	1 Fixed 2 Movable 11 Patent type	Open
Queen Alexandra Dock	31.7.1894	13.7.1907	52	6 Movable 8 Patent type	Open

There were also 76 general cargo cranes at the docks (70 hydraulic and 6 electric).

Courtesy Derek Robinson

Appendix C

The Rise and Fall of the Coal Export Trade at
The Bute Docks, Cardiff

Year	Tons	Year	Tons	Year	Tons
1839	6,500	1881	5,243,352	1923	8,540,167
1840	43,651	1882	5,626,906	1924	7,684,400
1841	87,170	1883	6,503,447	1925	6,620,392
1842	196,259	1884	6,773,189	1926	2,902,734
1843	210,655	1885	6,678,133	1927	7,290,586
1844	258,072	1886	6,521,956	1928	7,007,937
1845	359,755	1887	6,858,299	1929	7,211,609
1846	420,281	1888	7,604,856	1930	6,358,004
1847	441,073	1889	7,735,536	1931	5,375,254
1848	619,226	1890	7,420,080	1932	4,832,313
1849	635,115	1891	6,949,424	1933	4,574,525
1850	661,382	1892	7,323,095	1934	4,745,476
1851	707,520	1893	6,725,320	1935	4,866,094
1852	801,697	1894	7,668,606	1936	4,493,153
1853	834,221	1895	7,542,220	1937	5,429,848
1854	1,051,748	1896	7,690,205	1938	4,980,479
1855	1,084,536	1897	7,722,995	1939	5,228,056
1856	1,327,660	1898	5,652,666	1940	3,217,410
1857	1,440,679	1899	8,279,005	1941	2,151,182
1858	1,258,627	1900	7,549,312	1942	2,254,207
1859	1,506,651	1901	7,216,311	1943	2,160,677
1860	1,794,005	1902	7,090,291	1944	1,292,518
1861	1,903,911	1903	7,169,912	1945	1,007,687
1862	2,073,387	1904	7,490,481	1946	1,095,639
1863	2,222,253	1905	7,294,020	1947	640,789
1864	2,098,604	1906	7,935,490	1948	1,414,598
1865	2,217,063	1907	8,909,823	1949	1,580,459
1866	2,278,175	1908	9,017,603	1950	1,301,512
1867	2,275,917	1909	9,614,950	1951	920,381
1868	2,371,870	1910	9,501,960	1952	1,193,421
1869	2,121,256	1911	9,320,656	1953	1,279,924
1870	2,104,545	1912	9,601,648	1954	1,170,645
1871	1,864,594	1913	10,576,506	1955	780,560
1872	2,494,905	1914	10,278,963	1956	628,121
1873	2,440,682	1915	8,934,275	1957	532,781
1874	2,583,665	1916	8,634,234	1958	394,055
1875	2,774,958	1917	7,449,835	1959	407,719
1876	3,526,819	1918	6,129,835	1960	377,493
1877	3,981,910	1919	6,508,679	1961	330,582
1878	4,133,911	1920	5,255,971	1962	389,788
1879	4,336,518	1921	3,860,554	1963	519,908
1880	4,843,982	1922	7,104,412	1964	229,105

Notes Total coal exports for the years that Cardiff was officially a coal exporting port: 510,772,607 tons.

Small quantities of coal have been both imported and exported at Cardiff since it officially ceased to be a coal exporting port in 1964. This has generally been handled by conveyor belt between ship and quay.

Main Events in Connection with Coal Exports Table

1839	First (West) Dock opened.
1859	East Dock fully open.
1865	Penarth Dock opened (opposition for coal trade).
1870/1	Depression in trade.
1874	Roath Basin opened.
1887	Roath Dock opened.
1889	Barry Dock opened (main opposition for coal trade).
1898	Coal Strike.
1907	Queen Alexandra Dock opened.
1921	Coal Strike.
1926	General and Coal Strike.
1930–6	General depression in trade.

Outline Summary of Vessels Cleared from Bute Docks, Cardiff

	Steamers	Sailing Ships	Total
1870	763	6,129	6,892
1880	3,131	5,986	9,117
1890	6,062	3,191	9,253
1900	6,527	2,617	9,144
1910	8,527	1,312	9,839
1920	10,076	1,211	11,287

The end of the Coryton branch at 2m. 56ch., seen on the 17th April, 1986.
Bob Pugh